Chilling True Tales of Old Preston

Book 2

K.A. Johnson

**OWL
BOOKS**

First Published October 1991 by
Owl Books,
P.O. Box 60,
Wigan WN1 2QB

ISBN 1 873888 05 8

Set in Cheltenham 10.5 point on 12.25 point
via DTP with 800 d.p.i laser printer

Designed and typeset by Graphic Design Ltd, Wigan.
Printed and bound in Great Britain.

Like his predecessors, as far back as he can trace, Keith Anthony Johnson is a Prestonian. Born in the post-War baby boom, he was educated initially at St. Augustine's Roman Catholic School, before completing his studies at Harris College.

For many years he has had an avid interest in local history and in particular the lives of Preston people of a bygone age and is a member of the Lancashire Authors' Association.

Married with two young sons, he lives and works in the town as an engineering designer.

ACKNOWLEDGEMENTS

I am indebted to the reporters of the following newspapers who described the events that took place in great detail:

Preston Chronicle, founder Isaac Wilcockson (1812).
Preston Guardian, founder Joseph Livesey (1844).
Preston Herald, founder H.C. Barton (1855).
Lancashire Evening Post, founder George Toulmin (1886).

I further acknowledge the assistance given to me by the Harris Reference Library, Preston — they are quite wonderful.

Thanks to J.C. Fielding for the sketches that appear on pages 34, 61 and 86.

MAPS

Prelim IX — Guild Guide 1862.
Page 14 — Ordnance Map 1849.
Page 58 — Ordnance Map 1849.
Page 68 — The Guardian Map of Preston 1865.
Page 75 — Ordnance Map 1849.

BIBLIOGRAPHY

Whittle, P. *History of Preston* (1821).
Hardwick, C. *History of The Borough of Preston* (1857).
Hewitson, A. *History of Preston* (1883).
Griffiths, A. *Chronicles of Newgate* (1883).
Pilkington, W. *Then and Now* (1911).
Also
Souvenir of Preston Guild (1902).
Pictorial Guide to Preston (1913).
Illustrated London News (1842).

INTRODUCTION

This further collection of tales are every bit as real as the headline-making news of today. The incidents portrayed are typical of those enacted in any of the Lancashire towns caught up in the Industrial Revolution.

In 1866 an article appeared in the *Preston Chronicle* which gave a fascinating insight into life in 19th century Preston. The editorial appeared under the heading of Thievery, Knavery and Harlotry, in Preston and it included the following choice sentences:

"Crime is a gigantic stalking horse, always present in our midst, not easily removed, an object by which all are more or less affected. Every sensible man who will take the trouble to pry behind the scenes of daily life in our towns, cannot, I think, deny that our vast communities are falling from the paths of rectitude.

"Scarcely a day passes but one or more lads, hardly bordering on their teens, are brought up at our police court, on charges of pilfering. Boys, scarcely tall enough to see over the police dock, are arraigned for offences, which one would think they were hardly competent to commit.

"One cannot walk many yards in the streets but he meets with mere children the worse for liquor, or strutting about with short black pipes in their mouths, with their caps resting on one side of their head, addressing each other as 'chaps' and giving utterance to the most foul and horrible imprecations. One cannot raise his house windows without the breeze wafting in some of the most dreadful oaths and abusive epithets from the lips of mere striplings or grown up persons.

"One can scarcely pass along the streets with any article of value about him by way of outward decoration, but thievish eyes are upon them, and by the time he can cast his eye aside to ascertain if all is right, he finds himself relieved of his prizables.

"Whilst we can see parents with hoary locks and of all ages entering low taprooms, reeking with filth and tobacco fumes, while we can see them continually endeavouring to quench their liquor-parched throats, whilst we can see them staggering through the streets in a half-helpless condition, with their clothes torn to tatters, whilst we can hear them uttering the vilest of language, need we be astonished at the mental mediocrity and the thievish, knavish and blasphemous revellings of their half fed, half clothed offspring.

"One of the greatest evils with which a nation can be afflicted is that of harlotry. In Preston, like most other towns, the evil has made extensive strides, and yet nothing has been done to check it. Those set apart to carry out the law to the letter fail to do so in this respect, and wink at the existence of the crying evil. Seldom do we hear of the regulations being put into practise, and yet we have numerous notorious brothels existing in the very heart of the town; we have harlots prowling about our streets daily and nightly. Our principal thoroughfares are made parades for these nightwalkers, many of whom are mere girls, just entered their teens, entrapped by mistresses of brothels holding out to them great promises of reward.

"I question if vice is so prevalent among the savage barbarians as it is in our own country, and are there not vices to be found, at which a barbarian would almost blush with shame".

Strong words indeed, from a campaigning newspaper about a town, which according to a report in the same paper in 1861, had been dubbed a cotton factory town. The article had first appeared in 'The Builder' a national publication. A correspondent had visited the town and walking through the streets had made his obversations, writing as follows:

"Fishergate runs along a ridge and whenever there is a gap in the houses a view of the factories in the surrounding hollows is obtained. The factories are piled storey above storey, the tall chimneys keeping guard over all, and the squat houses of the operatives are spun out in rows around.

"Fishergate stretches out bravely before us with bonnet-shops, booksellers and bootmakers, side by side with the palatial Preston Banking Company premises which dwarfs its unpretending neighbours the chandlers, chemists, hairdressers, tailors and butchers shops.

"The market place is a handsome roomy parallelogram, surrounded on two sides by good shops, inns and hotels; by the Town Hall (a dingy worn-out mansion) on the third; and by a row of shops on the fourth, which is broken up by alleys leading to the Shambles at the rear of them. The gutters in the market place run with slops thrown out of the houses in the carts around.

"A long old-fashioned winding thoroughfare called Friargate, struggles downhill from the Market Place. This is a long and tortuous street of second and third rate shops, to supply the innumerable courts and alleys with which it is intersected. In the alleys and courts the laws of the Board of Health are set at defiance. The rear premises of both sides of Friargate are horrible masses of corruption and forcing pits for fever. Some of them such as Hardman's Yard at the corner of the newly-painted Waterloo Inn, are whitened and made showing to look clean about the entrances. But step past the whitewash near the street and you will find a master midden pit, with privies at each end, open to the front of a whole row of houses whose inhabitants they serve. Peelings, slops and tea leaves are strewn about the yard and the clothes of the poor people are hanging to dry over this disgusting pit".

The report continued in a similar vein, highlighting the problems of insanitary living conditions among the densely-populated town centre residents.

The townsfolk had to endure many traumatic periods during the development of the area and all-too-often the national situation influenced local life. The years just prior to the abolition of the Corn Laws by Sir Robert Peel in 1846, were particularly harrowing. They were dark days when the two pound loaf cost eightpence and women were heard to say: "Whatever shall we do now, bread is a penny a mouthful".

The food the working classes had to exist upon in the 1840s was such that the poorest amongst us would refuse today. The famine put the price of corn up, but wages remained stationary. It was meal and water porridge, three times a day, and by way of a change a plateful of thick porridge with black treacle in the middle. Men, women and children grew visibly thinner, yet they worked like slaves.

Labour was undoubtedly at the mercy of the capital and working men found it difficult to endure. The cotton factory operatives' lot was not a happy one, short time, stoppages, trade depressions, reductions in wages, lock outs. Workers were treated as nonentities, too ignorant to proclaim their own grievances and wrongs.

It is against this background that the tales unfold and what follows are real events that were in the minds and hearts of our ancestors.

Any judgement should only be made relative to the age in which they lived, a bygone era of trials and tribulations, far removed from our present day consumer society. The incidents that occurred gave common folk a strong and determined will, and they followed with great interest the events that unfolded around them. The community spirit was strong and great loss was felt when a tragedy occurred amongst them.

K.A. Johnson, 1991

Preston Market Place and Obelisk in 1830. This historic site has witnessed many dramatic scenes down the centuries. From ordinary Preston folk busily engaged in trade since being granted a free market by Royal Charter in the 14th century, to stirring scenes of civic pageantry.

On this site James I (1566-1625) (James VI of Scotland) was greeted by the Mayor and Corporation whilst travelling via the town in 1617, and here the Stuart Pretender — Charles Edward Stuart (1720-88) was proclaimed King. Here too the Guild Merchants' celebrations were once formally opened with a flourish of ceremonial fanfare.

The Market Place has also witnessed the darker side of man's nature through the pillory, which was last used in 1816 and the nearby parish pump which was regularly used as a whipping post to 'purge the souls' of wicked Preston men and women.

The Obelisk which had replaced serveral earlier market crosses was originally erected in 1782. It was dismantled in 1853 and removed to Hollowforth Hall, Woodplumpton. In 1979, to celebrate the town's octocentenary of the granting of the Charter by Henry II (1133-89), it was re-erected and now stands at the far side of the ancient Market Place.

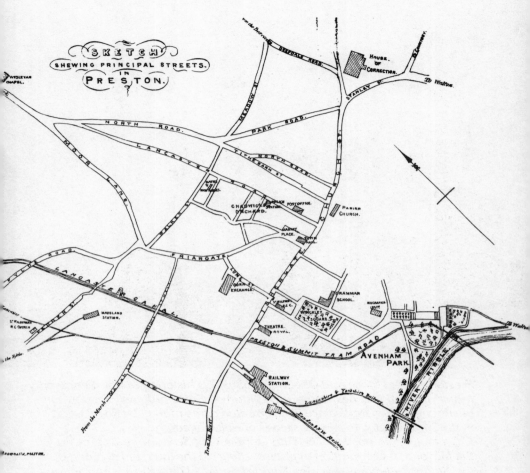

Principal street map of Preston, 1862

CONTENTS

"Mangled" Body Found in Bridge St.

ON Sunday, 2nd September, 1827, when the various congregations were at their respective devotions, the people in the neighbourhood of Bridge Street were thrown into a state of agitation and horror by the discovery of a sanguinary deed. It had been perpetrated in a house only six doors distant from the dwelling of the late John Scott and his wife, for whose murder, by poison, their daughter Jane was awaiting trial at Lancaster Castle. (The story of Jane Scott is related in *Chilling True Tales of Old Preston,* Book 1)

The victim of the shocking outrage was a man named Edward Gregson; about 60 years of age, he had the care of a small shop situated in Bridge Street, about halfway between Friargate and the Canal Bridge, where he lived alone. The shop had one window looking into Bridge Street, another pointing up the street and an outer door in the corner, between the windows. Gregson in his early life was a servant in the family of a Dr. Stapleton and afterwards was in a similar situation at Lostock Hall. He was a very honest and worthy character, and was placed in the shop by the owner of the premises, to carry on a small huckstery concern.

A little after ten o'clock that Sunday morning, according to his custom, Gregson's son called to accompany his father to the Roman Catholic Chapel. He found the door of the shop shut, fastened only by the latch. Having entered the house, he called several times at the foot of the stairs, but receiving no answer, sat himself down for a few minutes supposing his father had gone out and would soon return.

Then observing his father's shoes, he began to imagine that something was amiss. He therefore proceeded upstairs and was horror-struck by the dreadful spectacle that was presented to him.

There were two very small apartments above corresponding with the shop and in one of them young Gregson beheld the mangled body of

13

his murdered father lying upon the bed steeped in blood. He shrunk back with dismay at the sight and ran across the street to inform a neighbour of the dreadful circumstance.

The news soon spread; the constables were brought to the spot and an investigation instantly commenced to trace out the "murderous wretches" who had been guilty of the horrid deed. On examining the body of the unfortunate man, it was found that his skull was fractured, his throat cut in a shocking manner and various other parts of his body bruised and wounded. One constable then proceeded to examine the house, in order to discover, if possible, the instruments of death. In the apartment behind the shop he found a pair of tongs belonging to the house in such a condition which made it possible they had been used to effect the fractures and inflict the bruises. Many conjectures were soon hazarded to account for the deed but the affair was enveloped in obscurity.

The following day Thomas Miller, Esq., the Mayor of Preston, summoned a jury to investigate the case. From the depositions given, the

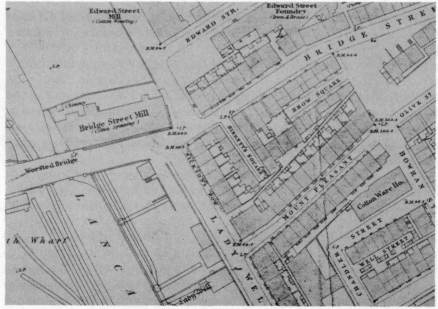

Bridge Street (now part of Marsh Lane), was the scene of the murder of Edward Gregson.

Entrance to St. Mary's Roman Catholic Church, Friargate, by E. Beattie 1894. Shortly after ten o'clock on the first Sunday in September, 1827, the son of Edward Gregson called to collect his father, as was his custom, to accompany him to the nearby St. Marys Church.

following emerged: On the Saturday night the deceased was left, about 11 o'clock, by his brother, son and son-in-law. A young man, a stranger to the latter three, but known to the deceased had also been in company with them. A suspicion was attached to this person as the guilty perpetrator of the deed, upon the ground of his mysterious appearance and equally unaccountable absence about the time when the horrid transaction took place. He had left the house at the time when the others parted and had not been seen or heard of since.

There were no circumstances positively fixing the time when the act was perpetrated, nor was it known how the guilty person, or persons, gained access to the premises. It was fairly evident from the circumstances of the deceased, being partly dressed in different clothes to those he had on when last seen, that he must have been to bed and was called up in the night or early in the morning under some pretence or other. There was no marks of violence to indicate that the premises had been forcibly entered.

On Wednesday, 19th September, the jury assembled once again at the Town Hall to proceed with the investigation relative to the murder of Edward Gregson. Thomas Miller, Esq., the Mayor, informed the jury that since they had last met a person had been apprehended who was suspected of being involved. That person was George Thornton aged 22, who lived in Savoy Street with his mother, a widow, his sister Ann, the housekeeper, and his two elder brothers; John, a shoemaker and Richard, a mechanic, who was in a poor state of health. George Thornton was trained as a fustion-cutter, but at the time he was apprehended he was unemployed, save for the assistance he gave to his brother, the shoemaker, binding and closing shoes. For three years he had drifted around, leaving Preston and returning on a number of occasions, his latest stay at home having lasted three months.

The first witness of the day was the suspect's mother, Elizabeth Thornton, who when she caught sight of her son exclaimed: "My blessed son! Art thou there! I have not seen him since he was taken. Poor thing, do they want to prove thee guilty of murder?"

She told the gathering that on the night of the outrage he was in bed by 11.30 p.m. and that she never heard him get up again. Evidence which was corroborated by his brother John.

A constable who apprehended the prisoner on Sunday, 9th September, stated that he had arrested him at the home of Thomas Ward, in Back Lane. He had told him he was being taken on suspicion of the murder of Edward Gregson, to which he had made no reply except that he had been at the house of Gregson on the night in question along with members of Gregson's family; having left about 11 o'clock.

The constable then went on to reveal that after locking up Thornton, he had gone to his lodgings in Savoy Street. There, on the bed of Thornton, he found a waistcoat and a pair of blue trousers. On inspection of the trousers the officer observed that the right hand pocket appeared to be smeared with blood and the front of the trousers looked as though blood had sprinkled on them.

Thornton's brother stated that he did his brother's washing and that he had not noticed any bloodstains on the articles in recent days. Concerning the bloodstained trousers he suggested that the blood could well have come from one of the many nose bleeds he was prone to.

Members of the Gregson family testified as to George Thornton being with them on the night before the killing — a fact which Thornton did not deny. While John Gregson, the son of the deceased, stated he had remained with his father for about 15 minutes after Thornton left, and that on going down Bridge Street, he had observed a man standing at the top of a narrow passageway on the opposite side of the street, looking towards the shop. He thought it was Thornton but in the moonlight it was difficult to see his features and as he got closer the person turned with his face towards the passage.

When all the evidence had been delivered the jury retired and they returned five minutes later to inform the coroner in the following words: "We are of the opinion that Edward Gregson was murdered by George Thornton, the person now before us".

The witnesses were then called and bound over to give their evidence at the assizes. The mother and sister manifested a strong feeling for their relative and against those who they considered were the instruments of his detention. The brother John attempting to pacify them by saying: "I'd rather George be sent to Lancaster, than be tried here". To which the mother, who originated from Lancaster, added: "Aye, they will do no harm to him at Lancaster; there was never a Freeman of Lancaster hung at Lancaster yet".

The prisoner though he seemed to feel the interest which his mother and sister took for him, sat throughout the investigation, in silent apathy, scarcely moving a single muscle, or appearing to take any material concern in what was going on.

In all, the inquiry lasted from ten o'clock in the morning, until six o'clock in the evening and when Thornton was conveyed back to the House of Correction, a vast concourse of persons followed the constables and the prisoner down the street, all eager to get a glimpse of the supposed murderer.

A couple of weeks after Thornton's remand, a man named Thomas Hansom caused something of a stir relative to the Bridge Street murder. Wandering about the streets on a Sunday night in a state of intoxication, he met three youths and told them he was the assassin who murdered old Gregson and that he had never been easy in his mind since. This fact was communicated to a constable who took Hansom into custody. On the following morning he expressed great surprise of what had occurred the night before and declared he had no knowledge of it whatsoever. The Mayor deemed it is duty to make a strict enquiry about the man, the result of which was that Hansom when in liquor was said to be little better than a lunatic. The conclusion being that there was no reason to suppose that his confession was anything more than the "wandering declaration of a disordered intellect". Hansom accounted for his occasional aberrations, by stating that he received a severe blow to the head when in the army at Quebec. The investigation completed, he was accordingly discharged.

The case against Thornton was scheduled for the Lancaster Lent Assizes of 1828. In the opening address of the Assizes, the Grand Jury were informed of difficulty with the charge relative to the evidence available. It was delayed until the end of the first week at which time the Grand Jury announced that they would ignore the Bill of Indictment preferred against George Thornton. The evidence being considered insufficient to support the charge.

Killers' Footprints
in the Snow

AT half past two on the morning of 11th November, 1862, Joseph Molyneux, a weaver, who resided at Ribchester, left his home to walk the 10 miles to Preston. It was a cold winter's night and snow and hail fell as he walked along. When he reached Grimsargh the road was white over and as he passed the local police station he observed four sets of footprints in the snow. The marks were not those of clogs, but of shoes and they could be clearly seen as near to Preston as Ribbleton Moor.

On the same morning at around six o'clock William Massey the head porter at Preston Railway Station, on the East Lancashire side, was on duty to supervise the first train from Preston. When he went to open the gates two men were standing waiting. They had obtained tickets from the booking clerk and their destination was Cherry Tree, near Blackburn.

Later that day news spread in Preston of a terrible murder at Ribchester, although the significance of these two occurrences and their ultimate connection was not to come to light for a number of weeks.

The victim was an old woman named Ann Walne who occupied a small old-fashioned public house known locally as the "Joiners Arms". It was situated on the southern side of the highway, midway between Longridge and Ribchester, on a stretch of road called Fleet Street Lane.

Ann Walne had been a widow woman for some twenty years and was reckoned to be about eighty years old. As a beerseller she commanded a good country trade which she ran with remarkable energy and skill. She had the reputation of being a careful, industrious woman; some would say a little miserly in her disposition. All who knew her were of the opinion that she had saved a great deal of money and that she generally kept a tolerably round sum in the house.

She was a woman of determined will and used to plod about from morning to night with surprising ease and with less exhaustion than many of younger years. She also had had three children during her lifetime but none of them lived with her during her later years. The old woman was a farmer as well as a beerseller, tenanting some land in the neighbourhood which belonged to a gentleman in Preston. On it she kept three or four cows and these were looked after by Joseph Ward, the labour master at Ribchester Workhouse. He used to attend the cows regularly night and morning, and was always ready to render her assistance when required.

On Monday, 10th November, after carrying out his usual shippon duties, Joseph Ward walked across the road to Mrs. Walne's house; it was about eight o'clock. In consequence of the weather having been very rough that night, she asked him if he would close the shutters for her. He did so, then left the woman in good health.

Shortly after six o'clock next morning, as was his custom, Ward went to fodder the cows. As he passed the house he noticed the shutters were not opened. This was unusual for generally the old woman was an early riser and as a rule was up by six o'clock in the morning.

After spending a few minutes busily engaged in the shippon, he went back to see if Mrs. Walne was up or not. He knocked on the house door but there was no response; the old woman had apparently still not risen. Returning to the shippon, he attended to his other tasks. On leaving the barn, he looked across the road and still noticed the shutters closed and the door shut. By this time, he was slightly apprehensive and resolved to knock at the door again. He did so. As on the first occasion, he received no reply. He then went home where he remained for a short time before returning to Mrs. Walne's home. On his arrival everything was still closed up and all appeared dark within the house. For the third time he knocked on the door but the result was the same. This time he was convinced that something was amiss; that the old woman was either dead or very poorly. After knocking at the door several times he went round to the back of the house. At the rear of the property he saw that the pantry window had been bodily removed. The window had been protected by three small iron bars inserted in the stonework. The bars had been wrenched away, the window removed and the woodwork and glass was lying on the ground broken to pieces.

Ward was greatly alarmed by what he had discovered and immediately ran off to the house of a neighbouring farmer for assistance. The two men at once returned to the premises and gained entry through the broken window hole. Several times they shouted out "Nanny", which was the name given to the old woman by neighbours, but still there was no reply. That there had been a robbery they were in no doubt and from the silence of Mrs. Walne they feared she had sustained some serious injury. It was clear she was not in the house part or the pantry, for they went into three places and looked them through. They then proceeded upstairs.

She usually slept in the middle room which fronted onto the road and they at once walked into that room. There were two beds in the room and lying on one of them was the almost naked body of Mrs. Walne. The bed clothes were arranged as if a terrible struggle had taken place. A shawl was placed over her face, and this was fastened down by another shawl which was tightly bound round her neck. She was "quite dead" and appeared to have been so for some time. Her arms were stretched out at full length and were fastened with handkerchiefs to the posts of the bed.

The two men immediately raised the alarm and the police soon arrived. After making initial enquiries, a man named Thomas Davis was apprehended. He was a returned convict and a former resident of Ribchester Workhouse. He later appeared at the inquest which was held at the Black Bull Inn, Ribchester, and was described as an elderly, shrewd and rather savage looking man. Dressed in plain fustian clothes, there was little evidence to implicate him with the crime, other than the fact that the day before the murder he had called on Mrs. Walne to enquire if she had any work for him that winter. Having been suspicious of him, she had sent him on his way. The inquest was adjourned however; the coroner thought it fit that Davis should be removed back to Ribchester lock-up.

In the next couple of days two other paupers from Ribchester Workhouse were apprehended on suspicion of being concerned in the murder. They were Charles Fishwick and Stephen Balshard, who were subjected to considerable interrogation. A magistrate of the county later ruled there was nothing proved against them and ordered their discharge and a further remand for Davis.

A week later the murder enquiry took a dramatic turn. Early on Sunday morning six men were apprehended in Blackburn on the charge of having murdered Mrs. Walne of the Joiners Arms, Ribchester and also with having entered her house with a burglarious intent.

On the following morning, the men, Duncan McPhail, a returned convict, William Woods, Daniel Carr, George Woods, Benjamin Hartley and Thomas Bowling were placed in the dock of the Blackburn Police Court.

Supt. Higgs of the county constabulary applied that the prisoner Bowling, otherwise known as 'Chorley Tom', who stated he was unconnected with the crime, should be discharged, as he was able to give some important evidence against the other prisoners. While asking for his discharge, Supt. Higgs also applied to have him bound over to give evidence against the other prisoners. The bench granted the request, whereupon Bowling was released from the dock and put into the witness box.

Bowling described as a notorious character, gave evidence that a short time after the murder he called upon McPhail, who lived near Belle Vue Gardens, Blackburn, and that whilst at his home he told him full particulars of the crime. The testimony of Bowling was of great

THE MURDER AT RIBCHESTER.

APPREHENSION OF SEVERAL MEN.
STARTLING CONFESSION.

Early on Sunday morning, six men were apprehended in Blackburn, on the charge of having murdered Mrs. Ann Walne, of the Joiners' Arms, Ribchester, on the morning of the 11th ult., and also with having entered her house with a burglarious intent. On Monday morning, the men, named Duncan M'Phail, a returned convict, William Woods, Daniel Carr, George Woods, Benjamin Hartley, and Thomas Bowling, were placed in the dock of the Blackburn Police Court, before Messrs. Baynes, Lund, and Johnston, on the charge. Mr. Superintendent Higgs, of the county constabulary, applied that the prisoner Bowling, otherwise "Chorley Tom," who stated to have been unconnected with the crime, should be discharged, as he was able to give some important evidence against the other prisoners. While asking for his discharge, he (Mr. Higgs) also applied to have him (Bowling) bound over to give significance and the men were all remanded while further investigations took place.

Eventually on Monday, 8th December, the case was fully investigated at the Blackburn Police Court. The proceedings were commenced in the small court; but the excitement was so great, and the crowd so immense that it was found necessary before the trial had proceeded very far, to adjourn to the large room.

Since the last proceedings the prisoner Benjamin Hartley had made a confession and Supt. McNab of the county constabulary told the court how Hartley had requested him to visit him in his cell and take down his statement. He then read the statement out to the court:

"The week before the murder McPhail came to me and said that he had been at Ribchester. He said he had called on the old woman who kept the beer house there (Mrs. Walne); that he had learned she had sold a cow, and had a considerable sum of money; that he was badly in want of money, and must have some. He said 'we must have it', and that he and me and Dan, and George must go. I said I cared nothing about it. He then told me that he had seen the others (meaning George Woods and Daniel Carr), and that we were to meet on Salford Bridge at six o'clock on the following Friday evening. On the Friday evening McPhail brought his 'trap' to Salford Bridge, in Blackburn, where we all met him. But we objected to go that night, as it was moonlight. We accordingly went home and as we were going we arranged to go on the following Sunday night. We met at Dan Carr's on the Sunday night, at seven o'clock. George Woods was drunk and we resolved not to go that night. We decided to meet again on the following Monday night and to go then, whether it was wet or fair. We had to meet at six o'clock. McPhail came to my house at six o'clock on the Monday night, the Monday night the 10th November. He said he had seen the others, and that they had gone on to Salford Bridge. We then set off together, and we afterwards met Daniel Carr and George Woods. Carr had a cane loaded with lead; George had another stick like it. He had also a crow bar with him. McPhail had a dark lantern and a pistol. I had no weapon with me..We met an old man there. I said, "Old man, it's roughish". It was hailing. He said, "Aye, it is". We went across Ribchester Bridge, and afterwards through Ribchester. When we went through Ribchester, we came to a place where they were building a cow shed. Some of them wanted to shelter there, but we decided not to do so, and went on. It struck eight after we had got over Ribchester Bridge. When we had got through the village, and past the new cow shed, McPhail said, "There's a footpath up to th'old woman's, let us take it; it'll be the quietest there". We accordingly went along the fields, and, as we were going along, we came to a barn. We sheltered there from about eight o'clock to twelve. McPhail had some rum with him in a bottle, and so had Dan, and we drank of it. We left there about twelve o'clock and then went to the old woman's barn, opposite her house. We lay down on some hay near the cows. When we had been there a short time McPhail said, "Come it's time to begin; let us go". He then went out, Carr followed him, then Woods, and afterwards myself. They told me to stand at the end of the house, to see if any one came up. Shortly afterwards, McPhail came up to me, and shouted out, "Come here, and I will get up the steps at the end of the house, and jump over". McPhail said they had got the window's out. He afterwards said, "Come, the window's out — in with you". George Woods got in first; I followed next. Then Dan struck a light and lighted the lantern and gave it to George. Then he and McPhail came in. McPhail and Dan were plundering about down stairs. George and I went upstairs. As soon as we went into the old woman's bedroom we saw her sitting up in bed. George said, "Where's thy money?" She made no reply, but commenced screaming. I then got hold of her and held her down on her back, and George commenced rooting about the bed. Then we went downstairs. I went after him. Dan and McPhail were at this time looking into the clock and the cupboard, and all round the house with a candle. The old woman was screaming and then George and I, and Dan went upstairs. I held the old woman down on the bed, and Dan drew out his cane, and said, "I'll make her make a less din" He struck at the old woman, but missed her. I had my left hand on her brow, and he struck it. I thought he had broken my hand. (Hartley had a bruise on his left hand, as if he had been struck there with some heavy, blunt instrument). I said to him, "Oh, dear, what art thou for". He replied, "Did I hit thee", and I said, "Aye". He then struck her twice on the side of the head and she cried out, "Oh dear me, you have killed me". George Woods held a light. We afterwards went downstairs and left her. When we had got down Dan said, "She must be tied". George Woods then got two handkerchiefs and he and I went upstairs and tied her hands. I said to George, "You must tie her, for I can't with my hand". While we were tying her down, Dan and McPhail were searching upstairs. The old woman was left when we tied her hands, and she kept moaning. We had no light when we tied her hands. We afterwards all went through the back window and out at a gate past some cottages. We went up through Longridge and on the road to Preston. Whilst on the way between Longridge and Preston and when on Ribbleton Moor, they took the lead off the stick. George put his lead into his pocket, and Dan Carr gave his stick to George afterwards. George took the lead off it, and then threw the stick away, McPhail and George went through some brick fields. I and Dan went on to Preston, and we stopped at a public house near to the House of Correction. It would be about a quarter past five o'clock when we got there. The public house was open, and we went in and got two glasses of whiskey each. We paid for our own in silver. We stopped there about half an hour, and then went to the railway station and booked for Cherry Tree Station, near Blackburn. We got off at Cherry Tree Station and walked forward to Blackburn. We separated at Bank Top and I went home. When we were on the road to Preston, George who had the money, said he had got about £40; but when he came to look at it he found that there was silver mixed with the sovereigns. He divided the money. I got four sovereigns and 10s. 6d. in silver. We all got the same. George said the money was lapped up in an old flannel. He threw the flannel away as we were coming along the road. McPhail and George said they would walk to Bamber Bridge, when they left us at Preston, and then get on the train. The day after I went down to Dan's. He told me that George and McPhail were off drinking and that they had hired a cab. Dan struck the old woman very hard, and made her head rattle. The crow-bar was thrown over a hedge on the left hand side, just where a gutter crosses the road, and not far from the old woman's house. Bill Lankey, flagger and slater, met us as we got out at Cherry Tree Railway Station. I have given this statement without any promise of reward. I have been very uneasy in my ease ever since, and I thought of making this confession before I was apprehended but I put it off until now".

Almost immediately, Hartley was committed for trial at the next Liverpool Assizes. Next, the court considered the case of William Woods, the brother of George Woods, one of the other suspects. It was decided that after what had transpired, there was no case against him and that he should be discharged without any stain upon his character.

Next it was the turn of Duncan McPhail, George Woods and Daniel Carr to face the glare of the court. McPhail was described as a smart looking fellow and Woods and Carr as plain every-day looking men — "not very bad in their appearance, and yet not over good".

Hartley was the first to give evidence against them and he repeated in the main the facts in his confession. Among the other witnesses called to testify, were Joseph Molyneux, the man from Ribchester, who, on walking to Preston in the early hours of 11th November, had traced the footprints of four men in the snow. Then William Massey, the head porter at Preston Railway Station, recalled the appearance of Hartley and another man at the station to catch the first train to Cherry Tree that morning.

The testimony of these men, and other witnesses, confirmed the truth of Hartley's confession. At the end of lengthy proceedings, the three men were committed for trial at the next Liverpool Assizes.

On the following Wednesday afternoon, the remanded men were conveyed by the three o'clock train, via Preston, to Kirkdale Gaol. The townsfolk of Blackburn were in an excited state and great crowds of persons surrounded the police station and lined the route to the railway station.

Carr, Woods and McPhail were conveyed together to the station and Hartley was taken in a separate conveyance with Supt. Higgs. A strong force of constables prevented any violence and the crowd "hooted" as the prisoners went by.

A local newspaper described the four men as follows:

> "McPhail about forty years old, had lately carried out the business of hawking cheese, bacon and greengroceries up and down the district. He had first come to note at Clitheroe, where he was sent to gaol for three months as a whisky spinner. He then went to Chorley and did business as a tailor and draper, before again returning to Clitheroe. Soon afterwards he was found guilty of perjury on seven counts, and committed for seven years transportation on each count. This was in 1852 and in 1855 he was liberated on leave. Some years after he commenced business at Witton as a coal dealer and failing, he started the business of hawking.
>
> "Carr said to be forty-five years of age was described as very short in stature, slightly marked with smallpox and forbidding in countenance. He had suffered two terms of four years imprisonment for manslaughter and robbery.
>
> "Woods was a discharged artilleryman, who had lately mixed with poachers and other undesirables.
>
> "Hartley was described as an unoffending man as far as crime was concerned. Prior to the present situation, he earned his living as a power-loom weaver"

On Monday, 30th March, 1863, Duncan McPhail and Woods appeared at Liverpool Assizes charged with the 'Wilful Murder' of Mrs. Ann Walne, at Ribchester. A second count of felony was included in the indictment. At the opening of the proceedings it was stated that Daniel Carr who was also committed on the same charge, had died in Kirkdale Gaol early that morning. For two or three weeks Carr had been in a nervous state. On the morning of the trial he had eaten his breakfast, and as he was preparing to go in the prison van to the Assizes, he fell back in his seat and died almost immediately.

Once again witnesses from the earlier committal proceedings were examined and they recalled the grim details of the crime. Both prisoners had competent defence counsel and when Hartley, the approver was called, they cross-examined him thoroughly. He stuck firm to his original statement, however, and the situation looked bleak for McPhail and Woods.

In their summings up, the defence counsel suggested that much of the evidence of Hartley was uncorroborated. Both suggested that there was a lack of positive identification of their clients.

When His Lordship summed up, he came down strongly against McPhail and concluded by telling the jury to reach a verdict that the evidence and the circumstances of the case demanded.

After a lengthy absence the jury returned with a verdict of 'Guilty' against both prisoners, with a recommendation to mercy.

His Lordship then put on the black cap and in a solemn silence, pronounced sentence of death, without any hope of mercy, upon the prisoners.

The prisoners were then removed. McPhail appeared to be in a weak and nervous state and looked pale, while Woods maintained great calmness and firmness with only a melancholy look upon his face.

The following morning Benjamin Hartley, the 'approver' appeared in the same court room on a charge of murdering Ann Walne. He pleaded Not Guilty and there being no evidence offered by the prosecution, the jury at once acquitted him.

That night a great crowd was waiting at Blackburn for his arrival by the last train from Liverpool. The police thought it wise to delay his return home and when he arrived at his home in Pearson Street, Blackburn, on the following Wednesday afternoon, a number of constables were in attendence. Once again a great crowd gathered and yelled their disapproval of the part he had played in the Ribchester tragedy.

The front of his home was daubed with various slogans including "Hartley, the Ribchester murderer". The bailiffs were soon in possession of the house, and at about three o'clock a cab arrived to convey Hartley and his wife to his sister's home in Preston. The mob yelled fiercely as he entered the cab and with his sobbing wife beside him, he was conveyed with great speed up Chapel Street and towards the railway station.

'Chorley Tom' also made a brief appearance in the town and he also was given a rough reception on account of his disgraceful conduct in the affair.

The *Preston Chronicle* in its editorial was highly critical of the affair and the leniency shown towards Hartley—commenting as follows:

"Hartley, the approver—evidently one of the greatest villains in this foul drama of murder—has been discharged. He has been a mean fellow and a coward in the whole transaction; for he not only did his share in the murdering business, but afterwards "split" not because his soul was awed with the terrible character of the tragedy, and not because he desired justice to be done to the guilty, but because he wished to save his own wind-pipe at the expense of his companions' necks.

'Chorley Tom', who asked for a share of the plunder, and then told the police who the murderers were, is also no better than he should be. The best thing which could be done would be to hang the whole troop; nobody would miss them, and everybody would feel that they had got rid of a bad, rascally tribe of plunderers".

In the weeks prior to their executions, efforts were made to save the lives of McPhail and Woods and memorials were sent to the Home Secretary, Sir George Grey. McPhail even made a confession in which he claimed that the actual killing had been the work of the other prisoners. Wood responded in reproachful terms to the statement made by McPhail and stated that certain deeds attributed to him by McPhail were in fact done by McPhail.

On the Thursday morning before the executions, a reply was received from the Home Secretary, which stated there was no reason to interfere with the carrying out of the extreme sentence of the law.

When Saturday arrived, crowds of people began assembling in Liverpool, many of them having travelled on foot from Blackburn, Chorley,

Preston and other Lancashire towns; for the passion for witnessing hanging was still great. As noon approached an estimated 50,000 persons were outside Kirkdale Gaol. The vast crowd included persons of all ranks, grades and colours. There were soldiers and sailors; mechanics in their greasy suits and labourers in their white smock coats; old men on the edge of the grave and youths full of fun and nonsense; ladies in fine clothes shutting out the sunlight in their expensive hats and silken parasols; old women, advanced into grey hairs; little children, dressed in motley rags; servant girls who had come for the sight and sensation; and country youths who had travelled miles to view the cold horrors of the strangulation.

Shortly before twelve o'clock, the outer door leading to the gallows was opened. The executioner was William Calcraft. The crowd stood in silence as he appeared on the scaffold with the condemned men. The Rev. Appleton read the usual service as Calcraft went about his business. Firstly he attended to Woods, whose features although wan and pallid, were calm and composed. He had walked to the drop with a firm and determined step. Calcraft fixed the rope upon his neck, drew up the noose, attached the hook at the higher end to the chain above, pinioned his feet and covered his face.

The executioner then attended to McPhail, who seemed rather agitated and filled with nervous apprehension. After the pinioning process had been completed the white cap was drawn over his face. Remarkably, Calcraft then shook hands with both men and stepped back from the scaffold.

The bolt was drawn and Woods and McPhail were very soon into eternity. Woods never moved at all, he fell heavily and appeared to die instantaneously. McPhail struggled rather severely for about half a minute, and his head was thrown considerably to the right. At first his movements were strong but gradually got weaker, and in less than a minute he was in the grasp of death.

After being gazed upon by a considerable crowd, at the termination of one hour, Calcraft removed the suspended corpses from the drop.

Calcraft, the 'Short Drop' Hangman

William Calcraft was the last officially appointed hangman of the City of London. The man he succeeded as official executioner was Foxen who he had become acquainted with during 1828. His first meeting with Foxen took place in Finsbury Square early one morning in that year.

Calcraft had seen Foxen leant against a lamp post, coughing violently, and his kindly nature led him to invite the distressed man to enter a neighbouring house and take a little peppermint. Foxen informed him that he was the executioner and that he was on his way to Newgate to hang a man. He told Calcraft that his cough was getting so much the master of him that he feared he would not be able to carry out his duties much longer.

When he explained to Calcraft that there was no apparent successor to him, as his assistant, Tom Cheshire, was given to drink and not trustworthy, the eager young Calcraft replied "I think I could do that sort of job".

Within twelve months William Calcraft was the official executioner and his chance meeting with Foxen had played no small part in his selection.

It was customary during that period to make the executioner take the Bible in his hand and swear solemnly that he would despatch every criminal condemned to die, without favouring father or mother or any other relation or friend. When he had taken the oath the hangman was dismissed with the words: "Get thee hence,

William Calcraft, official hangman from 1829 to 1874.

wretch!"

For his exertions Calcraft earned a guinea per week (21 shillings) and an extra guinea for every execution. He also received half-a-crown for every man he flogged and was given an allowance to provide cats or birch rods. He was at liberty to engage himself in the country, where he demanded and was paid £10 on each occasion.

In his official capacity Calcraft was a regular visitor to Lancashire, following the trial judges on the Assizes circuit.

The executions of Duncan McPhail and George Woods at Kirkdale Gaol brought back memories of his previous visit, in the autumn of 1862, when he also performed a double execution. On that occasion in excess of two hundred constables were employed in ensuring his protection after a threat to his well being had been made.

Little could be done to intimidate him however and six months after despatching the Ribchester murderers, he was back at Liverpool to 'drive more immortal souls into eternity'. On that occasion he built a scaffold to accommodate four men and in his own unswerving manner he ended the existence of a Spanish seaman, a wife killer, a Welsh sailor and another seafarer.

His visits to Lancashire were not however always so 'fruitful'. Indeed in 1862 when engaged to visit Lancaster Castle to hang convicted killer Walker-Moore, a tailor from Colne, he had to endure a wasted journey. Having carefully prepared the scaffold, he was informed just hours before the appointed time, that the convicted man had cheated the gallows by committing suicide in the water closet.

Described as an illiterate, simple-minded man, he scarcely remembered what executions he had performed. He kept no record of them and when asked questions referred the enquiries to the officers of the gaol.

In his later years when he went to the prison for his wages he was often accompanied by his grandchildren, who affectionately held his hands. He also was often seen being followed by his pet pony which trailed him round like a dog.

Calcraft was regarded as not unskilful in the hanging profession, but he was said to proceed by rule of thumb, leaving the result very much to chance and the strength of the rope. He was much in favour of short drops and there were undoubtedly failures. The common custom was for him to go below the gallows "just to steady their legs a little"—in other words to add his weight to the hanging bodies.

In all, he served the City of London until 1874 when he was pensioned at the rate of twenty-five shillings per week. His death occurred peacefully five years later at Hoxton, near London, on 13th December, 1879 aged 79.

A Victorian engraving of Calcraft flogging one Bernard Regan in 1871, a duty for which he would have received half-a-crown.

Mrs. Black, the Jewel Thief

IN the summer of 1862, one year after Fulwood Barracks had been the scene of the murder of Colonel Crofton and Captain Hanham, it once again hit the headlines.

Captain Bluett, a member of the 10th Regiment, announced that a quantity of jewellery had been stolen from his possession. As a result he had a bill printed offering a reward for their recovery. The jewellery noted missing was a massive gold serpent ring, set with a topaz of an elongated shape, a gold ring with three light coloured rubies, a gold ring with three large turquoise, a gold ring set with one sapphire and two pearls and a gold necklet with an amethyst in the centre and rubies round it.

In September of the same year around the time of the anniversary of her husbands death, Mrs. Crofton, the widow of Colonel Crofton, discovered that a diamond ring had gone missing from her jewellery box. Placards were immediately put out and a reward offered for recovery of Mrs. Crofton's ring.

As a result of these thefts a thorough investigation took place which resulted in the eventual arrest of a Mrs. Jessie Black, the wife of Captain Black, who at the time of the disappearance of the jewellery was stationed at Fulwood Barracks. Mrs. Black was brought up on remand at the House of Correction in March, 1863, charged with stealing a quantity of jewellery, the property of Captain Bluett and Mrs. Crofton.

Regarding the jewellery belonging to Captain Bluett, a great deal of evidence was stacked up against Mrs. Black. She had often been a visitor to Mrs. Bluett's quarters and had on more than one occasion been in a position to have taken the missing items. Also various witnesses testified as to her possession of the jewellery, including a pawnbroker from Leicester, to where she had removed after parting from her husband.

Mrs. Crofton was examined and she testified as to the disappearance of her diamond ring in September, 1862. Once again the court heard how the jewellery had been discovered in Leicester.

Witnesses testified to Mrs. Black having possession of the ring, which was a diamond half hoop, with stones down the centre. One jeweller recalling how he had offered Mrs. Black £20 for it but she had declined the offer claiming it was worth twice that amount. A pawnbroker from Golden Square, London also gave evidence. He told the court that the ring had been pledged with him a couple of times. On the first occasion Mrs. Black had sent it to him by letter from the Victoria Hotel, Fulwood and on the second occasion from a Leicester address. The ring had been pledged on both occasions for a sum of around £15.

When all the evidence had been submitted Mrs. Black was asked if she had anything to say in answer to the charge. She made no answer, and was committed for trial at the forthcoming Liverpool Assizes.

A couple of weeks later she appeared before Judge Baron Martin at Liverpool on the indictment of robbery of jewellery, the property of Mrs. Crofton and Captain Bluett. She immediately pleaded guilty and was sentenced to eighteen months imprisonment. The following week's editorial in the *Preston Chronicle* was highly critical of the lightness of the sentence imposed on Mrs. Black commenting as follows:-

"Mrs. Black appeared like a lady. She had the education of a lady; she associated with ladies; but it was all outside work. Her fine feathered hat, and her grand sealskin mantilla, and her long silk flounces, all covered up the corruption within. She could talk French and God knows what besides; but she didn't understand that English version of that plainest of commandments 'Thou shalt not steal'—rumour says that there were other parts of the decalogue which she did not care about also. she was a lady in appearance; but at heart was as false a jailer and as crafty a siren, as ever visited the scene of her thieving—Fulwood Barracks. I've no patience with these fine delinquents. Easy minded, well to do folk, who make a curious distinction between crimes committed by the rich and those perpetrated by the poor, call her 'unfortunate' I call her a fine rogue, well up in trickery and thoroughly acquainted with all the secrets of long-fingered dodgers. She was false from her feet to the crown of her head, for she wore long, heavy, massive trusses of raven hair, which even made the barristers in court grow amorous; but it all meant nothing more than a wig. If I had been Baron Martin, I should have opened her fine dark eyes far wider than he did with the sentence of the

Judge Baron Martin was critcised for the lenient sentence imposed on jewel thief Mrs. Black.

Law. If some ugly washer-woman, or some servant lass in a printed gown, had done the same thing, that hard judicial Irishman would have administered a far severer penalty than he did in Mrs. Black's case; I think so, at all events his leniency is a marvel; but perhaps he imagines that he will see her again during his rounds.

Death of a Prizefighter in The Shambles

S HORTLY after six o'clock in the evening, on the last Tuesday in April, 1848, Thomas Ellis, the keeper of the Golden Cross beerhouse, in The Shambles area of Preston, was in the vault of his establishment. Sharing a glass of ale with him was James Townley, another local beerhouse tenant. As the two men stood chatting at the bar they were joined by James 'Touch' Duckworth, a well-known local man, who worked as a horse breaker and livery stable keeper.

Duckworth, a man in his forties, shook hands with Ellis and Townley and the landlord treated him to a glass of ale. All three men were far from sober and after a time Duckworth began to argue that Townley owed him some money. Townley, in turn, denied any such debt. Ellis was anxious that a row should not develop in his vault and attempted to intervene. The response of Duckworth, who had a reputation as a bare knuckle prizefighter, was to invite Townley into the yard to fight for a round or two.

Despite Duckworth's reputation, Townley felt honour-bound, to accept the invitation and made his way into the yard. Fearing for Townley's chances, innkeeper Ellis intervened and managed to persuade him to return to the vault. As Townley walked back through the vault door he was met by a young man named Richard Catterall, a local plasterer, who was keen to know what the commotion was about.

When Townley told him that Duckworth had been asking him to fight him, Catterall responded by saying: "I'll go and fight him". He was soon out in the yard telling Duckworth that he wished to fight him. Duckworth was reluctant to fight Catterall, having no quarrel with him, but Catterall was insistent.

The Shambles, Lancaster Road which was demolished in 1896 for the building of Miller Arcade. In April, 1848, James Duckworth, a man with a reputation of a prizefighter was sent sprawling back onto one of the stone pillars in The Shambles during a deadly drunken brawl.

He began squaring up to Duckworth and eventually Duckworth responded by removing his hat and coat and a cigar from his mouth, saying to Catterall: "Then damn you, I will fight you, if you'll fight fair up". The two men then appeared to be squaring up to each other when Catterall suddenly rushed forward and grabbed Duckworth round the thighs running him backwards. The thrust by Catterall sent Duckworth sprawling back on to one of the stone pillars which projected out from the row of butchers' shops which stood along one length of The Shambles.

The lunging attack by Catterall was a fatal one, the impact of contact with the pillar causing considerable damage down Duckworth's right hand side, including the fracture of four ribs. These ribs, in turn caused severe lacerations to the liver and internal bleeding.

In severe pain, Duckworth was assisted to a nearby house followed by a distraught Catterall, who was rubbing his hands and saying "Oh, Duckworth, don't die". But Catterall's pleading was in vain. Within a few minutes Duckworth was dead.

When the inquest into the death of James Duckworth was held on the following Thursday afternoon, both Richard Catterall and James Townley were seated in the dock. However as the proceedings developed, it became apparent that Townley had not been a party to the actual killing of Duckworth and he was liberated. For Catterall it was only the latest stage in his ordeal, with the inquest jury returning a verdict of 'Manslaughter' against him after a few minutes deliberation. That same evening Catterall was taken to Lancaster to await his trial.

That trial took place at the Lancaster Lammas Assizes in August, 1848. Mr. Justice Cresswell presided over cases in the Crown Court. The criminal calendar was a light one, by normal standards, and only 18 cases and 22 prisoners were presented for consideration, the most serious crime being that of manslaughter.

The 23-year-old Catterall was said to have been "reeling drunk" at the time of the incident, according to the first witness called, who was Thomas Ellis of the Golden Cross vaults.

Indeed as the evidence was once again revealed, it became apparent that all the parties in the sad affray had been somewhat the worse for drink. The defence claimed that since the prisoner was drunk at the time he could not be guilty of manslaughter. His Lordship however saw the case in a different light, pointing out that the two men agreed to fight, they did fight and one being killed the other was guilty of manslaughter.

The Grand Jury spent little time before returning a verdict of Guilty of Manslaughter against Catterall. His Lordship then addressed the prisoner, commenting that "here was an instance of one of the lamentable consequences of drinking". He did not think that in the drunken brawl the prisoner contemplated doing the deceased any serious harm. Therefore considering the length of time that Catterall had been in custody already, he sentenced him to one month's imprisonment only, with hard labour.

Postscript :

Some fifty years later when recalling the old days an elderly Prestonian had this to say about 'Touch' Duckworth. "He was a man who was at once the terror and delight of the town. After living in St. John's Street and Tithebarn Street, he went to live in a warehouse close to the Parish Church. There in his cellar he kept a much talked about bear, with which on one occasion he terrified the bailiffs".

Arson Attempt in Tenterfield Street

IN the autumn of 1873, James Woodall a 37-year-old lamp and oil dealer of Preston, was in business from two different addresses in the town. In Orchard Street he had a shop from which he carried out his retail business and in nearby Tenterfield Street he had a shop with a dwelling house of two-storeys. On each side of the brick built premises were wooden sheds which were used mainly as warehouses, with the back portion used as stables for his working horses.

In the Orchard Street shop, Mr. Woodall was assisted by William Cawthorne and his wife Emma. The couple resided over the former shop in Tenterfield Street and with their daily duties over, returned there each evening. The other employee of the business was a 14-year-old named William Parker, whose role was that of errand boy.

Just before eight o'clock at night on the 27th October, 1873, the boy was instructed by Mr. Cawthorne to go to one of the sheds on an errand. As he entered the lock-up shed he noticed at a distance a faint light flickering between a pile of crates. Moving closer he observed a crate filled with straw and perched over a paraffin-wax candle. The candle, stood inside an empty lucifer matchbox which was surrounded by a large quantity of cotton waste and straw.

The boy examined it no further, but thinking it a curious circumstance, immediately went to inform Mr. Cawthorne. Accompanying the boy into the shed Mr. Cawthorne observed that the light, the matchbox and the waste were all saturated with oil. The paraffin candle, which was one that burnt for six hours, was within an hour's burning before it reached the matchbox.

Mr. Cawthorne at once extinguished the candle and left the place, not knowing what it meant, but thinking it was a most extraordinary thing. He was soon discussing the matter with a gentleman from a neighbouring shop and instantly the pair returned to the warehouse.

They found nothing more in the room downstairs, but on ascending the second storey they saw a feeble light against the wall. The arrangement was precisely the same as downstairs, with the paraffin candle within an inch or so of touching the matchbox in which it was placed. Further investigation revealed another similarly concealed candle and it was apparent to the men, that had these devices not been discovered, within half-an-hour the whole place would have been ablaze, and the shops, sheds and neighbouring premises burnt down.

J. WOODALL & Co.,

PUBLICANS and the TRADE SUPPLIED.

GLASS,

CHINA, AND EARTHENWARE DEPOT,

LAMP AND OIL

MERCHANTS,

WHOLESALE & RETAIL.

LAMPS and **OILS** of every **DESCRIPTION.**

10, Orchard Street,

PRESTON.

The evening's events led to the appearance of James Woodall at the Manchester Assizes in December, 1873. He stood accused before Baron Pollock of attempted arson. The indictment to which he pleaded 'not guilty' consisted of several counts, charging him with having attempted to set fire to a warehouse in his own possession and his own property. Under such circumstances that, if the building had been set fire to, the offence would have amounted to a felony, with intent to injure and defraud.

Early on the morning of the alleged offence Mr. Woodall was said to have informed his staff that he was going to Liverpool for a couple of days. However various witnesses, including the errand boy, recalled seeing Mr. Woodall at the Tenterfield Street premises during the day. In his possession he was said to have had the very articles so strategically placed to ignite the blaze.

The prosecution informed the court that the Tenterfield Street buildings were insured in two offices, one of the insurances being taken out three months before the alleged offence and being for £1,750. This insurance covering the wooden sheds £250, oil £50 and £1,450 for the glass and warehouse stock. The other insurance policy of longer standing, being one of £250 on the brick buildings, making a total insurance of £2,000.

With the stock estimated at £1,750 the prisoner appeared to be under insured, but the prosecutions theory was that Woodall was anxious to obtain the £2,000 insurance money to enable him to leave Preston and set up in business elsewhere.

When the defence counsel rose to address the Court he claimed that the prisoner would have been a loser by pursuing such a course of action as the prosecution suggested. Mr. Woodall, he told the jury, was a prosperous tradesman who occupied a most respectable position. To claim the insurance money instead of disposing of the goods to customers, would have made Mr. Woodall a loser.

There was not a shred of motive the defence claimed, and some other person could well have concocted the whole affair. Who had set the candles alight was open to debate he added, and his client was entitled to any doubt which existed.

When His Lordship summed up the proceedings he reminded the jury that it was a very serious crime and needed to be weighed seriously. The jury then retired to consider their verdict and the prisoner who had appeared calm and collected throughout was ordered to stand down.

After an absence of a little over half-an-hour, the jury returned and the prisoner stepped into the dock, with visible anxiety upon his face. The verdict of the jury was guilty and when asked if he had anything to say why sentence should not be passed upon him, he made no reply.

His Lordship addressed Woodall in a serious tone, and said that it was a melancholy thing to see a person who had occupied his position in life, in the dock of a Criminal Court, charged with a crime that was so clearly and manifestly proved. He then reminded him that purely for commercial gain he had contrived to set fire to his own and adjoining buildings which were filled with human beings. He finished by informing Woodall that the decision of the Court was that he be kept in penal servitude for a period of five years.

Catastrophy at Brunswick Mill

PRIOR to the summer of 1848, Preston was justifiably proud of its record in respect of industrial accidents. Despite being one of the north's fastest growing industrial towns, it had managed to avoid the fearful catastrophies that had occurred in other towns. Therefore when in June, 1848, a boiler explosion occurred at the Royal Sovereign Mill, and seven lives were lost, a great gloom was cast over the local population. Sadly, before that gloom had cleared, and while the towns-people were still subscribing to a benevolent fund for the relief of the surviving relatives of the deceased, a further catastrophy was to strike the town.

The date was Monday, 31st July, 1848. The scene of horror was Brunswick Mill at Lambert Bottoms, which was in the ownership of Messrs. John Cooper and T.J. Garrington. Situated in a dell at the north east corner of the town, the factory was a few hundred yards north west of the House of Recovery. It was a small and comparatively old concern which was originally occupied by Francis Lambert, hence the name of its location. The business had been in the possession of Mr. Cooper and his junior partner for some nine years.

It had been just another Monday morning for the mill's workforce and as lunchtime approached all were busy at their labours. The mill had on its lower floor, a boiler house which contained two boilers, while the second floor consisted of a mechanics shop and counting house at the front, with the remaining area consisting of a reeling or winding room. In it were six reeling frames, which when the mill was in full production, were operated by twelve females.

Suddenly, without warning, at 25 minutes past eleven that forenoon, disaster struck. Without warning one of the boilers burst, thrusting forward from its seat some $7^{1}/_{2}$ feet. As it did so the steam connnecting pipes above it ruptured the ceiling which formed the floor of the reeling room. At the same time all of the brickwork around the boiler was thrown down together with the plate between the two boilers, the hopper (or fire-feeding apparatus) and the mercury gauge. The boiler house being thus strewn with fragments of brick, iron, flags and other debris. A quantity of the projected fragments alighted in the yard, and some were even carried against the opposite row of cottages, a distance of eighty feet, breaking several windows. The entire area of the ruptured portion of the reeling room floor was about thirty two square yards. The planks and joists being forced upwards in several places and the room filled with a dense volume of steam.

The sound of the explosion was heard about a quarter of a mile away and the females in the reeling room shrieked with horror as the floor parted and a great rush of steam entered the area. Disaster had struck and the *Preston Guardian* gave a comprehensive account of the unfortunate occurrence which left, seven dead and four injured. The report gave the following particulars:

KILLED:

1. **William Middleton,** aged 48, of Brown's Yard, Friargate. He was engaged in re-setting the brickwork around the adjoining boiler, which had been repaired. He was thrown forward about seven feet, and when found was almost completely covered with bricks, bits of flag and other debris which had been cast about by the explosion. He was at that time quite dead, and he had received several severe contusions, especially at the back of the head. The deceased was well known in the town, and left a wife and four children. He had only arrived that morning to the work on which he was engaged, having previously been occupied at Mr. Goodair's mill.

2. **Robert Wilkinson,** aged 46, of Lambert's Bottoms. Wilkinson, having just made up his fire a few minutes before the bursting of the boiler, ascended into the reeling room, as he was sometimes in the habit of doing, to get a pinch of snuff. For this purpose he beckoned to Betsy Lambert, who was working at the first reeling frame, and who generally carried a box. He took the snuff, and descended into the boiler house and in less than two minutes the explosion was heard by the girls above. Wilkinson could therefore only have been descending the steps of the boiler house when the boiler burst. He was not injured by any of the projectiles, but was blown down into the corner below the steps and dreadfully scalded. He, however, was able to ascend the steps, open the boiler

house door, and walk to his own house near the mill. He was met at the end of the mill by his wife, to whom he exclaimed: "O, Mary, pray for me. I'm done for now!" He was able to walk up to his bedroom, where his clothes were removed. He presented a frightful spectacle and was scalded over the whole person. He was however, perfectly sensible and collected, and during the afternoon he made statements as to the cause of the accident to several individuals including his medical attendant Mr. Halden. He died at five minutes to five that fateful Monday afternoon, leaving a wife and five children, three of them married.

3. **Thomas Hardman**, aged 36, of Kirkham Street North. He was a fellow workman with Middleton and was also engaged at the time of the accident in resetting the brickwork on the adjoining boiler. According to Woods a labourer who was just leaving the boiler house, Hardman was last seen along with Middleton, although the former was thrown by the force of the steam in a different direction to the latter. He was not injured by any materials dislodged by the bursting of the boiler, but was dreadfully scalded on the back and the neck. He managed to walk to his own house and Mr. Booth, the surgeon, was immediately in attendance upon him. He died, however, about seven o'clock the same evening. He was described as a very worthy and steady man. He left a wife and two young children, one just seven months old. His parents also, both of whom were supported by his industry, were said to have been left destitute.

4. **Mary Hart**, aged 20 of 92 Back Lane. When the explosion occurred she was at work in the reeling room and was very severely scalded. She was removed along with Ellen Robinson, her companion at the frame, to a neighbouring house and later to the House of Recovery. She was scalded chiefly on the face, arms, legs and upper portion of the back. Besides the external scalding she suffered greatly from respiration problems caused by the sudden entrance of steam into the throat. Eventually at twenty five minutes past six o'clock that Monday evening, she passed away.

5. **Mary Jackson**, aged 24, of 113 North Road. A married woman, she was also a reeler in the upper room and was moved about one o'clock to the House of Recovery. She was chiefly scalded about the arms and face. Her greatest problem however, was the inhalation of the steam and this caused so great a difficulty of respiration as to induce frequent spasms. She lingered in excessive agony until five minutes past five the following morning. Immediately after her death, a Caesarean operation was performed on her in an attempt to save the child she was far advanced in carrying. Sadly the

operation was unsuccessful and Mary Jackson left behind a husband and one child living.

6. **Sarah Hesketh**, aged 38, of Lambert's Bottoms. A single woman she was at work at the fourth winding frame at the time of the explosion. She instantly rushed to the front, and leapt from the door above the boiler house, spraining her ankle on alighting. She was taken in a fly to the House of Recovery at one o'clock and died at a quarter before one the next morning. She was less severely scalded than any of the other deceased, the injuries being confined chiefly to her arms. The shock she had sustained, however, from her fright and fall proved too much for her, and she never rallied despite the application of stimulants.

7. **Jane Carr**, aged 39, of Atkinson Street. A married woman, she was working as a winder at the furthest frame in the room, nearest the portion of the floor ruptured by the explosion. She was consequently exposed to the strongest volley of steam, and had the greatest difficulty reaching the door. She was carried to the House of Recovery about half past one o'clock and died in less than two hours. Her whole body was scalded and considering her condition all were astonished that she survived even for a minute. She left two children and a husband who was working abroad.

INJURED:

1. **Betsy Lambert**, aged 30, of Lambert's Bottoms. Married with two children, she was the woman whom engine-tenter Wilkinson has solicited a little snuff from, a minute or two before the accident. Shortly after Wilkinson's departure, the females in the winding room felt the floor vibrating beneath them, and the room instantly filled with vapour. She instinctively thrust the cop- bag she held in her hand against her mouth, in order to exclude the steam from her throat. By doing so her arms were exposed to the steam and considerably scalded. She rushed to the door and leapt down the steps in front of the factory.

2. **Ellen Robinson**, aged 22, of Lambert's Bottoms. A married woman, she was at work on the third frame at the time of the accident. Hearing the explosion and feeling the vibration of the room she instantly hurried to the front part of the building, and boldly leapt from the door of the mechanics shop. She injured her ankles by the daring act, but was scarcely touched by the steam. As a result she looked forward to a complete recovery within a few weeks.

3. **Betsy Helme**, aged 19, of 107 North Road. This girl was rather severely scalded about the face, neck and upper part of the back,

arms and hands. However it was hoped that with medical care a gradual improvement would be made in her condition.

4. **Mary Ann Harrell**, aged 20, of Chatham Street. She worked at the second reel and both her arms and her face were severely burnt. She was taken to her own residence in a fly, and there was given constant medical assistance. Opinion was that given time she would recover from her terrible ordeal".

Besides the tragic tale of those who suffered the ravages of the boiler explosion there was also the tale of those who escaped the disastrous occurrence.

In all seven other persons four females and three males, accidentally escaped. There were generally twelve females occupied in the reeling room. Of these, one named Mary Ann Longworth, was unwell and absent, a second, Elizabeth Hesketh, lately married, was not at work in consequence of her reel being broken. A third, Margaret Farnworth, had just left the room to pay some money to the officer of a local burial club and the fourth Mary Wright, had just left the room to prepare dinner for her mother, who lived in an adjoining cellar.

The three males who escaped were James Wood, labourer, William Taylor, mechanic, and a youth named Christopher Holden who was employed as a book-keeper. Woods, had just left the boiler house. Taylor had been out repairing a shutter near the mill, and was returning at the time of the accident. While Holden had left the counting house for some purpose or other immediately before the accident.

On the following Wednesday afternoon at the Town Hall the inquest into the accident was held before the coroner Richard Palmer. The court was crowded during the investigation, with the concourse of curious onlookers extending into the street. The proceedings began at three o'clock and after details were given of the seven deaths, an extensive investigation was made into the cause of the tragedy.

Boiler maker Joseph Clayton told the inquest that on 3rd July, he had made a temporary repair of the boiler. One of the stays was broken and Mr. Fogg, the manager of Brunswick Mill, had requested that he attend to it. He was questioned as to the general safety of the boiler and he told the hearing that in his opinion it was not safe to operate at the pressure it was being worked at. Having repaired the stay requested by Mr. Fogg, he had during the following days replaced two more stays and fitted a strap under the bottom or bridge of the boiler.

A great deal of discussion was held over the boiler's capacity and it was stated that by area of surface and construction it was capable of driving a twenty six horse power engine. However the boiler was being worked to a pressure capable of working an engine of forty or forty five horse power. It was apparent from the proceedings that Mr. Fogg had been warned as to the dangers involved in such a practice, yet had seen fit to have the "boil-over pipes" removed in order to achieve the pressure required. The boiler had been continually worked at the excessive pressure which exceeded all bounds of reason for a waggon-shaped boiler.

It was apparent that over a period of time the work at the mill had exceeded the power of the engine. Consequently the practice of working the lower pressure to a higher pressure was resorted to. It was a reckless practice and one which daily carried the risk of an accident.

Mr. Clayton recalled how he had been called to a meeting with Mr. Fogg at which he had told him that the waggon boilers were unsuitable for driving the engine and that moves should be made to replace them with circular boilers.

Shortly after nine o'clock in the evening the coroner sent the jury out to consider their verdict. They returned into the court room at ten o'clock and the foreman announced the following verdict "Accidental

Brunswick Mill at Lambert Bottoms, was the scene of a dreadful catastophy on the last day in July, 1848. B B are the arched entrances of the boiler house which contains two boilers, the one on the left hand being that which burst. C is a small counting-house above, and M another small apartment, about seven feet wide, for the repairs of tools, &c., by the mechanic. With the exception of these small rooms in front, the whole of this storey consists of a reeling or winding-room. This is filled with six reeling frames, at which twelve females are generally engaged, but at the time of the explosion there were only eight at work. D is the door of the mechanicss' shop, but its also accessible from the reeling room.

Death" caused by the bursting of the boiler. The jury are unanimously of the opinion that considerable blame is attached to the engineer and manager in working the boiler at a higher pressure than it was calculated to bear.

The *Preston Guardian* and many of the townsfolk were far from happy with the jury's verdict and mounted a campaign to have the accident further investigated. As a result a meeting was held a few days later in the Town Hall and a request for a further investigation was sent to the Home Secretary, Sir George Grey.

After a letter of acknowledgement was received, a further communication followed, addressed to the Mayor of Preston. It read as follows:

Whitehall 15th August, 1848

Sir — I am directed by Secretary Sir George Grey to inform relative to the recent boiler explosion at Preston, that, the Law Officers of the Crown are of opinion, that an indictment of manslaughter should be preferred against Fogg, the manager of the mill, and the Solicitor to the Treasury has been instructed to proceed accordingly.

I am sir, your obedient servant

H. Waddington

As a result Roger Fogg appeared at the South Lancashire Assizes on the last Monday in March, 1849. He was charged with causing the death of Mary Hart, and the others, in consequence of the explosion of a boiler of which he had the management. The history of the boiler was once again thoroughly discussed and the removal of the "boil-over" pipes. When His Lordship Baron Alderson discussed the evidence he reminded Fogg that his negligence had caused the death of Mary Hart and others, who had met with a painful and premature end. He also stated that his employers had acted improperly as they appeared to have allowed the working of the old engine in order to save their pockets the expense of a new one.

To this suggestion the defence counsel stated that it was not to save the expense but the reverse, claiming that for many months before the explosion the mill had been working at a loss merely to keep the hands employed.

With the jury returning a verdict of 'Guilty of Manslaughter', His Lordship addressed Roger Fogg in the following manner: "I trust that what has transpired in this case will be a warning to others in situations like that of the prisoner. In order that it may be a lesson to others the sentence of the court is that you be fined £5 and enter into your own recognizances of £100 to be of good behaviour for two years.

After consenting to enter into the recognizances and paying the £5 fine, Roger Fogg was discharged.

The sentence far from pleased the *Preston Guardian*, who suggested that his doubtless respectable exterior and religious membership, which were largely dwelt upon by the counsel for the defence, had carried their due weight in mitigating punishment. Five pounds they continued, is the price for smashing a lamp and causing a street row. Five pounds is little more than the cost of a game certificate for killing hares and pheasants. Five pounds is a mere bagatelle; and yet five pounds is the price for killing seven human beings by an act of recklessness, not casual but habitual.

Whether Fogg or his employers should have been in the dock was another debatable point according to the newspaper which suggested as the judge inferred that a considerable portion of blame lay on their shoulders.

One pleasing feature of the court case was the fact that His Lordship said that the survivors of the deceased had every right to expect from the employers the fullest possible compensation.

The newspaper was also constructive in suggesting that a regulation ought to be adopted to prohibit all workshops immediately above boiler-houses. Pointing out that it was hardly pleasant for a lot of workpeople to be standing ten hours a day over an iron volcano, as the poor girls in the Brunswick Mill were doing.

No Reprieve for Thomas Riley

THOMAS Riley, who hailed from Bradford, came to Preston during the time the Park Hotel was being built and followed his occupation as a stonemason. He was a widower with four children, one of whom also came to Preston to take up employment in the town.

During his stay in Preston, Riley made the acquaintance of Elizabeth Alston, who lived in a small cottage at 10 Back Dock Street. She was the wife of Christopher Alston, a labourer, who during the time the acquaintance between Riley and the woman commenced, was working at Grimsargh and came home usually once a week, leaving sufficient to maintain his wife during the intervals between his periodical visits.

The acquaintance was formed unknown to Elizabeth Alston's husband and on occasions he fetched her beer from the Bay Horse Inn which was situated nearby. On the 27th of September, 1883, Riley and the woman, having been drinking together several days, were seen in a state of intoxication. The woman was worse for drink than he, and was in such a state at five o'clock in the afternoon, that she could not stand without support.

Some four hours later a neighbour heard talking and singing in the house which Mrs. Alston occupied and could distinguish two voices. She heard no scuffle and no screaming, and there was nothing noticeable beyond what was ordinarily heard in that house.

A little later on, Thomas Norcross who was on his way home, and lived at 9 Back Dock Street, met Riley leaving the house of Elizabeth Alston. Norcross shortly afterward left his home and went to the Bay Horse Inn. He was told when he got there that Riley had been in a short time before and putting his hand on the counter, had left the marks of what appeared to be blood.

What the landlady told Norcross induced him to go to Mrs. Alston's house. On arriving there he struck a light and found the woman apparently asleep, lying on the floor, in what he thought at the time was a pool of water. It was about this time that Riley, going to the house of a woman named Taylor, exclaimed that: "Liz was proper drunk, lying on the broad of her back and that he could not waken her". Mrs. Taylor, with another neighbour, went to the house and it was then that the true state of Mrs. Alston was discovered. She was lying, not in water, but in blood and was dead.

Mrs. Taylor went for a constable and on walking with him down Fishergate they met Riley, who was coming out of the North Western Hotel, and who exclaimed: "Is she dead?" On Mrs. Taylor's replying: "Aye, she's dead enough", he proceeded voluntarily with the party to the house, and sat down on a chair.

The Park Hotel, overlooking Miller Park (now Lancashire County Council Offices). It opened in 1882. Among the tradesmen employed on the construction of this building was Thomas Riley, a stonemason from Bradford.

51

He was afterwards taken into custody, and on being examined, blood was found on his trousers and shirt.

On Thursday, 8th of November, 1883, 55 year old Thomas Riley appeared at the Manchester Winter Assizes accused of the wilful murder of Elizabeth Alston. To the charge Riley replied "I am not guilty, I never did it".

The doctor who examined the body of Mrs. Alston described the wounds inflicted on her as of a horrible nature. Looking round the room to see if he could find anything that might have caused the wounds. He had discovered a shovel which had a handle stained with blood. He noticed that there were marks or scratches on the deceased's eyelids, cheeks and nose, and bruise marks on the back of each hand.

When the defence addressed His Lordship and the jury, he remarked that he could not find out how the prosecution connected the prisoner with the murder, except that he was supposed to have been the last man with the woman. Concerning the shovel, he said he couldn't see why the shovel should not be found with bloodstains upon it considering it had been lying on the floor all the night before.

His Lordship, in summing up, told the jury they must consider the case dispassionately. If the woman, as it had been suggested, had fallen by accident, a single fall would not have caused all those fearful injuries described by the doctor. Nor was it conceivable that such injuries could have been self-inflicted. He then charged them to carry out their duty regardless of anything, except the desire to ascertain the truth.

The jury retired to consider their verdict at two o'clock in the afternoon and some ten minutes later they returned to the box. The Foreman of the jury, in answer to the Clerk, stated they had found a verdict of 'Guilty'. The prisoner who was much affected, muttered: "I did not do it".

The Judge, having assumed the black cap, proceeded to pronouce the sentence of death. He said: "Thomas Riley, you have been found guilty of a most barbarous and atrocious murder. I can find no words to express the feelings which have pervaded me, and, I am quite sure, everybody who has listened to this painful trial. It would serve me no good if I were again to enter into the harrowing details of your crime. I have only to tell you that for that crime you must die. The law commands me to pass upon you the sentence of death. This is not the time, and I am not the man, to advise you how to seek for pardon from Almighty God, whose laws you have so grievously broken. I have only to pass upon you sentence of death. In the prison to which you will be conveyed, you will have every assistance which a man can have in making your peace with Almighty God and praying for pardon".

He then pronounced sentence of death in the usual form. The prisoner seemed to feel his position acutely during the trial. Being rather deaf, he strained every nerve to catch what was being said by the counsel and the witnesses. Indeed, at his insistence, Major Preston, the governor of the gaol, interrupted the Judge when he was passing sentence and said the prisoner could not hear. His Lordship repeated what he had already said in a louder tone of voice and Riley then seemed to comprehend the full solemnity of the situation. He made no demonstration of feeling on hearing his fate, and pensively allowed himself to be removed from the dock.

The verdict of the jury did not meet with the approval of a good many people in Preston, and a petition was made to the Home Secretary, praying that an inquiry might be made into the case, which it was hoped, would result in a reprieve for the convict. Mr. Halewood, of Friargate, was the prime mover in the matter and in the petition that was framed it was set forth that the convict was the first to draw attention to the deceased after her death, that the act (if done by him), was apparently done without malice and that the Coroner's Jury returned an Open Verdict. The petition, though only open for signatures for two or three days, was signed by over 7,000 people, including town council officials, several magistrates, doctors and lawyers. Attention was drawn to the fact that a witness at the coroners inquest had testified that she had handled the bloodstained shovel while attending to the deceased, was not called at the trial, and the petitioners tried to make the most of this circumstance.

At mid-day, on the last Saturday in November, the Home Secretary sent a telegram stating that he thought himself not justified in advising Her Majesty to interfere with the due course of the law.

This decision came down on Riley like a thunder clap, though he had been warned not to nourish any vain hopes. In the condemned cell he had maintained a cheerful and hopeful demeanour, and had expressed to his relatives the belief that he would be reprieved. When the fatal news was broke to him he lapsed into a feeling of resignation.

On the Sunday, he attended the morning and afternoon services in the prison chapel and in the evening, appearing in a composed state, he reiterated that he was not guilty of the crime. He slept soundly during the night and the ringing of the prison bell at six o'clock on the morning of the execution failed to awaken him. He rose shortly afterwards and dressed. A little later he was joined by the chaplain, who remained with him reading and praying until the appointed hour.

About five minutes before eight o'clock Bartholomew Binns, the executioner, entered the cell, and pinioned the convict. As he was passing the strap round his elbows, Riley exclaimed: "Don't tie me so tight lad".

Preceeded by the chaplain, who recited passages from the burial service, Riley walked firmly along the short passage leading to the scaffold, which was on the same level as the cell. Binns was immediately behind, and following him were the governor of Strangeways Gaol and other prison officials. As he left the cell Riley, who was evidently in great distress, said to the chaplain. "This is very hard". He also muttered something else, which was understood to be: "All for nothing". He was quickly placed on the trap of the scaffold, and at that moment appeared to waver a bit. The cap and rope were adjusted and the bolt was withdrawn. A drop of seven foot was given and death was instantaneous.

Shortly after the execution notices were placed on the gates of the prison, one being that the convict had been executed according to law, and the other a certificate of death signed by the prison surgeon. The black flag had been hoisted a few minutes after eight o'clock and this was the signal to a few groups of people in the street that the commands of the law had been fulfilled.

A couple of days later a letter appeared in the *Preston Guardian* expressing the view of a number of the town's residents:

PRESTON MURDER CASE
To the Editor of The Preston Guardian

Sir, — Would you allow us space in your paper, to thank those kind friends who so generously responded to our invitation to sign the petition on behalf of Thomas Riley. To Mr. Halewood, Friargate, we award the Hon's share of this merciful glory. To His Worship the Mayor (Mr. Forshaw), and his brother Magistrates, to the various members of the Town Council, and to the leading Tradesmen generally we bestow our special thanks. And to the 7,000 and upwards of inhabitants, we give our heartiest thanks for their great kindness. In conclusion we sincerely hope that the time is not far distant in this country, when men may have fairer trials than Riley had. — Hoping you will find space for this, we remain yours truly,

Thomas Houghton, Bay Horse, Pitt Street.
John Singleton, Grocer, Pitt Street.
James Pickup, Grocer, Bow Lane.
Edward Hardman, Bow lane.
Nov.26th, 1883.

Postscript :

By a singular coincidence, when Riley stood on the gallows, it was exactly two years to the day after John Aspinall Simpson had stood in the same spot, to be executed for the murder of Annie Ratcliffe, the daughter of the landlord of The Bluebell Inn. (See story 'The Slaying of Annie Ratcliffe' *Chilling True Tales of Old Preston* Book 1).

Escape from the House of Correction

IT was announced in 1789, that the new concourse of buildings at the eastern end of Church Street, were ready for occupation. They had been built upon the plan of the celebrated philanthropist and prison reformer, John Howard and the town welcomed its new House of Correction.

The buildings for reception of criminals, were surrounded by a three tier high boundary wall; with a governor's residence, large sessions house, wings containing ground and attic cells, weaving shops, hospitals and a chapel. The prison was an impressive self- contained unit.

Down the years various wings containing additional cells were added and the prison was reported upon favourably by the various prison inspectors. One of whom made the following observations:

"Convicts upon their entry are taught to weave cotton so that in the space of one month they are generally able to earn the whole amount expended for their food. With the exception of invalids, there are no idle hands within the prison.

"The prisoners work ten hours daily in summer, and six hours in winter, certain intervals being allowed in the course of the day for meals and recreation.

"It is necessary that prisoners who work hard should be well fed. This is the case at Preston where every individual has the following:

"Twenty ounces of good bread daily, besides a quart of gruel for breakfast, and the same for supper and for dinner a quart of soup, which on certain days of the week is exchanged for a moderate allowance of boiled beef and potatoes, or of cheese.

"The sleeping cells in this prison are ranged on one side of long corridors, which open on the other to the external air. Thus, these cells are very airy. They are provided with good bedding and like the rest of the prison, are in a condition of much cleanliness.

"The prisoners are also properly clothed when they continue for any length of time in the prison. They are bathed occasionally and their linen is changed weekly".

In the year 1848, a young man named Thomas Dewhurst, who could neither read nor write, was destined to sample prison life in Preston's House of Correction. Found guilty of stealing pigeons at Galgate, he was sentenced to be confined in the House of Correction for twelve months.

Prison life was not to the liking of this 21-year-old, and on the last Monday in April, 1848, news spread through the town of his daring escape. That Monday morning he was confined alone in the corridor sleeping block and managed to force back the lock of his cell door. This done he let himself out of the outer door which was unlocked and made his way to the cook-house which was also unsecured.

Once there he helped himself to some food and exchanged his clogs for a pair of wellington boots belonging to one of the cooks. Outside the cook-house he found a ladder and with some planks that were in the yard he raised it a sufficient height to reach the top of the wall. As he climbed the ladder he had in his hands some strong cording which had been used for laying out the grounds inside the prison. Doubling the cord up he secured it at the top of the wall and carefully lowered himself down the outside to freedom.

He was well on his way before his escape was detected and the Governor of the prison Colonel Martin informed. An immediate search was conducted for him and there were sightings during the day on the road to Liverpool and that night back in Preston.

On the Tuesday afternoon a robbery took place at St. Michaels, near Garstang, that was to provide the next link as to the whereabouts of the escaped convict. A dwelling house was broken into and various items stolen including a silver watch, wearing apparel and twenty shillings in silver. Immediately after the robbery, the property was missed, and information given to the police.

The search for Dewhurst was continuing and when on the Thursday afternoon two suspicious characters were detained by the police at Kendal; the pursuit was over. The two men identified themselves as John Buck and William Chadwick, on the former was found a watch, a bundle containing wearing apparel, a pawn ticket for a pair of trousers and five shillings and seven pence. Quizzed as to his recent activities he finally admitted that he was the escaped prisoner Thomas Dewhurst.

House of Correction. *Situated at the eastern end of Church Street the House of Correction was opened in 1789. In 1817 an extension for accommodating additional prisoners was built. It was reckoned that in the 1820s about one thousand persons passed through the House of Correction in the course of a year. Various other alterations followed including the construction in 1832 of the four martello towers, erected to "protect the prison from threatened attacks by mobs of machinery-breaking operatives". Three of the towers were demolished in 1864 and the fourth pulled down some thirteen years later. In 1878 the House of Correction as a prison was transferred from the Magistrates of the County of Lancaster to the Government.*

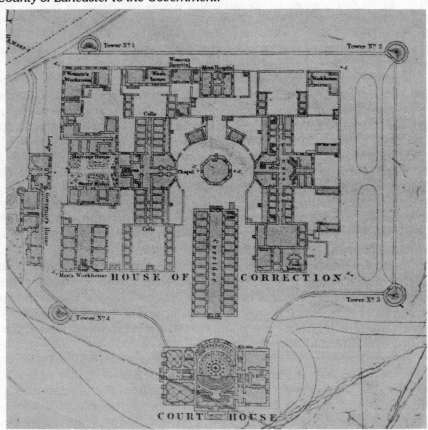

Plan view of the House of Correction taken from the 1849 map of Preston. It was on the last Monday in April, 1848, that Thomas Dewhurst made a daring escape from within its secure walls.

The Superintendent of Kendal Police escorted the two men to Preston on the following day, and they were confronted by a servant from the house that had been burgled at St. Michaels. He identified the coat that Dewhurst was wearing as belonging to him and also the silver watch, two silk handkerchiefs, two waistcoats and a couple of pairs of trousers found in Dewhurst's possession.

Dewhurst declined to say anything, but Chadwick volunteered to speak. He claimed he had met up with Dewhurst the evening after the robbery and that he had travelled with him northwards.

On Thursday, 18th May, 1848, the Intermediate Sessions for Preston started: Thomas Batty Addison was the chairman. The first day was drawing to a close when the charge against Thomas Dewhurst was entered. He pleaded guilty to stealing at St. Michaels and a list of items taken by him was read out. His escape from prison was recalled and his eventual recapture within a few days.

The chairman addressed Dewhurst in a stern manner reminding him that he had committed a determined and desperate robbery. With great deliberation he had found the means of setting himself at liberty from prison, but he had been careless of the course he took in order to enable himself to get away.

A convict in the Preston House of Correction in the 1820's was allowed the following provisions per week:

	s.	d.
Seven Loaves of bread, each weighing 20 ounces, and costs 13s. 9d. for every 100 loaves, will be nearly	1	0
One Pound of beef, costs 4d. per pound	0	4
Three quarters Pound of stew, costs 2d. per pound	0	1½
Two Pounds of oatmeal, costs three half pence per pound, or 30s. per load of 240lbs.	0	3
Quarter Pound of cheese, costs nearly 6d. per pound	0	1½
Quarter Pound of salt, costs 4d. per pound	0	1
Two Pound of potatoes, costs quarter per pound, or 5s. per load of 240lbs.	0	0½
Total per head weekly	1 11	½

Lancashire County Council Museum, Stanley Street, Preston, once Preston Court House, where Thomas Dewhurst faced chairman of the sessions, Thomas Batty Addison, on a charge of pigeon stealing

Continuing, he told the prisoner, it is necessary to make an example, in order that prisoners might know that when they are sentenced to a certain punishment, they must submit. In this case a severe punishment is necessary, as an example to others. He then announced that the sentence of the court was that Thomas Dewhurst be transported for seven years to parts beyond the sea.

Postscript:

The following January, Thomas Batty Addison made the news in *The Times* It reported on a trial that took place that month at the Preston Quarter Sessions. A woman named Mary Richardson had been charged with stealing half a crown from a labouring man at Chorley. The man swore that having gone out of a public house where he had been drinking; he felt a hand in his pocket where the half-crown was, and that the woman Richardson was the only person near him at the time. He took the woman into the public house, but she denied the theft.

She was, however, taken into custody and a quarter of an hour afterwards the half-crown was found about two yards from the spot where the man had been standing.

Upon this evidence the Jury returned a verdict of "Not Guilty". At this Thomas Batty Addison responded by saying: "Why this woman has been convicted before, and imprisoned in Lancaster for two years. A set of stupid fellows like you cannot see the evidence".

The remarks caused a great sensation in court and other members of the bench demonstrated their objections to the chairman's comments.

Thomas Batty Addison Recorder of Preston made an example of Dewhurst and ordered him to be transported.

The woman was then set at liberty and Mr. Addison stood accused of impropriety in the discharge of his judicial functions. He rode the storm of criticism and spent a further 25 years as Chairman of the Quarter Sessions. Resigning eventually in April, 1874, just two months before his death at the age of 86.

The Insurance Agent's Policies of Death

ON 17th September, 1877, Edmund Bennett, an insurance canvasser, who lived in Richmond Street, Preston, set off on the road to Longridge, in an attempt to obtain some clients for The Prudential Assurance Company. When he reached Alston he knocked at the door of the cottage home of Mary Whiteside, and his salesman's patter was successful. By the time he left, Mary Whiteside had agreed to take out Life Insurance Policies on herself, her husband Robert, her two children, John and Peter and her sister Ann Weighill. Little could Edmund Bennett have known when he clutched the signed proposal forms in his hand, that within a year, three of the persons whose lives were insured would be dead. Nor could he have imagined that the woman, whom he had just met, would be standing in the dock of the Crown Court of Lancaster Assizes accused of murder.

The policies were duly taken over by the local agent, James Cook, who resided in Berry Lane, Longridge, and he regularly called at the Whiteside's home to collect the premiums.

Early in the year of 1878, tragedy began to befall the Whiteside family when their two-year-old son Peter was taken ill, dying on 26th January. Within a matter of weeks his elder brother John, aged 5, was also taken ill and his death occurred on 7th April. Both deaths were attended to by the local practitioner, Edmund Eccles, who signed the death certificates.

After both deaths, the father, Robert Whiteside, called upon the local insurance agent James Cook and was paid the six pounds due upon the surrender of the policies.

The next significant event to take place occurred on 28th June of the same year. That day, Robert Whiteside, who was a strongly-built man some 5 feet 8 inches tall, worked in the gardens of Hothersall Hall, where he had been employed for the previous 15 months. He was in his usual good health and in a cheerful, good-spirited mood. His day's work over, he returned home and poured himself a glass of nettle beer. After which he ate his tea, which consisted of bread and butter followed by a large helping of gooseberry tart. He then sat upon the sofa nursing the baby for a short time.

Suddenly he was seized with a fearful pain and began shivering. He kept jerking his head backwards on the sofa, whilst his body kept convulsing upwards. His wife immediately ran for assistance and a local constable and a neighbour entered the house in an attempt to administer relief to him. He was offered a drink of water but refused and his face was wiped with a wet cloth to remove the perspiration from his brow.

His cramped position on the sofa was uncomfortable and he was laid on the floor. He then became quiet and within minutes he was dead. When Dr. Eccles arrived he gathered as much information as he could as to the cause of death. It was hot weather at the time, and from the information he received, he came to the conclusion that the man had died from sunstroke.

Before her husband's funeral, Mrs. Whiteside called at the home of the Insurance Agent James Cook to claim the money due on the death of her spouse. She told him that death had occurred due to apoplexy, accelerated by excessive heat. Within a few days she produced the necessary death certificate and Mr. Cook advanced her £3 on account for the policy which was for a sum of £7 15s.

Rumours abounded in Preston and Longridge and an Inquest into the death of Robert Whiteside, which returned a verdict of death by strychnine poison administered by persons unknown, failed to quell them. The fact that Mrs. Whiteside had lost two small children and her husband within a matter of months fuelled the rumours and they increased when it became common knowledge that on a number of occasions she had called at the local druggists in Longridge to purchase rat and mice poison which besides starch, liquorice and indigo contained the deadly strychnine.

With a view to dispelling the innuendoes, the respected Preston surgeon, Edwin Moore, was commissioned to carry out an examination on the body of Robert Whiteside in Longridge churchyard. The body was removed from the coffin and was found to be in a decomposed state. The surgeon removed various organs from the corpse and placed them in jars for later examination. The heart appeared healthy as did the liver, kidneys and other organs and nothing in their appearance seemed to account for his death. The theory that Robert Whiteside had died from apoplexy or from sunstroke was dismissed by Dr. Moore, and after consultation and examination of the organs by himself and a surgeon from Liverpool, a common conclusion was reached. That was the man had died as a result of poisoning by strychnine. This opinion was supported by the symptoms exhibited by the deceased, such as calling for air, shivering and shuddering, and remaining conscious up to the time of death. The fact that strychnia was not later found in the stomach, did not alter the opinion of the medical men. They were happy to refer to previous known cases of strychnia poisoning, where post-mortem examinations had failed to find any grains of the deadly substance.

As a result of the investigations Mary Whiteside appeared at Lancaster Assizes in January, 1879, accused of the murder of her husband the

An 1882 advertisement for the Preston branch of Prudential Assurance, the office from which insurance canvasser, Edmund Bennett was employed.

previous summer. The court was crowded for the hearing of the case and many were unable to gain admission. Mr. Justice Lindley presided over the proceedings and the jury were asked to dismiss from their minds anything they may have read in the newspapers with reference to the case.

The sequence of events that led to Mary Whiteside's appearance in the dock were revealed to the court. On 21st January, 1878, the prisoner had visited a chemist and druggist's shop in Longridge and purchased a 3d. packet of mice and rat poison, which contained sufficient strychnine to poison ten human beings. On the 26th of that month the little boy, Peter, just two-years-old, died and the insurance was obtained by the father, in the presence of the prisoner.

Then on 4th April, the prisoner visited the same druggist and purchased another packet of mice poison. Three days afterwards the boy John died and the policy money was paid to the father.

At about five o'clock on the 28th June, Mary Whiteside again visited the druggist and purchased another similar packet of poison. Within three hours Robert Whiteside, a strong muscular man, died in "excruciating agony", showing all the symptoms of poisoning by strychnine.

Edmund Eccles, who issued the death certificate stated that having heard the evidence and opinions of the medical experts called, he no longer held the view that the man had died from sunstroke.

It was testified that just half-a-grain of the poison would be sufficient to cause death, and various theories were suggested as to how it could have been administered. Half-a-grain dissolved in half a pint of water would cause a very bitter taste was the general opinion and for it to be consumed in an ordinary meal without detection was considered to be highly unlikely.

The question remained by whom was the deadly poison administered? There were only two conceivable administrators, the prisoner or the victim. In the case of the children, there was nothing to indicate they had died of poisoning. Although the circumstances and coincidences surrounding the situation inevitably led to the arousing of suspicions.

When His Lordship drew the investigation to a close, he told the jury that they must not convict the woman on circumstances alone and that it was their duty to decide whether the man was poisoned by strychnine. If they were convinced so, then they must find the prisoner guilty.

The jury retired, and after an absence of two hours and ten minutes returned into court. The verdict they brought with them was "Not Guilty" and Mary Whiteside was discharged on the indictment of murder.

The following day she once again appeared in the Lancaster Crown Court charged with feloniously endeavouring to obtain £20 17s by means of a forged death certificate. Mr. Justice Lindley once again presided, and Edmund Bennett, the insurance canvasser from Preston told the court how he had visited Mrs. Whiteside and she had agreed to take out the policies including one on the life of her sister Ann Weighill.

The policies were issued in due course and 3d. per week was paid to the agent on that policy which was the concern of the court hearing. Around Christmas, 1877, Mary Whiteside told a neighbour that her sister had died, and she borrowed money from her so that she might attend the funeral. She then visited the home of the Insurance Agent in Longridge and informed his wife that she wanted the money due. The agent's wife told her that she would not receive any money from such a new policy unless death had been caused by typhus, scarlet fever or something of that nature.

Mary Whiteside then went away but returned on 3rd January, with a certificate that stated that Ann Weighill had died of Bronchitis and Typhus Fever and it bore the signature of a doctor from Lytham.

The certificate aroused suspicion due to the misspelling of certain words. Subsequent investigations showed that no such Doctor Foster practised in Lytham, and indeed Ann Weighill was alive and well completely oblivious to her apparent death.

By eleven o'clock in the morning the jury had retired and when they returned after an absence of 22 minutes, the Foreman announced that they found the prisoner "Guilty as charged".

His Lordship then addressed her stating that she had been found guilty of an act of much deliberation, not something done on impulse. He then informed her that she was sentenced to 12 months imprisonment with hard labour. She was then taken to the cells below and the business of the Assizes was declared to be concluded.

Wife Killing in Ormskirk Road

HENRY Ashworth, a brewer by trade of Smith Street, Preston, appeared in the witness box of the Crown Court at the Lancaster Spring Assizes of March, 1865. He was there to recall the events of a September morning the previous year, and used the following words:

"On the morning of the 13th September last, I was in Bishopgate, leading out of Ormskirk Road. I had been helping to load a cart. About half past five I heard a scream, and went in the direction of the sound. I saw a woman at Leach's door in Ormskirk Road; she was bleeding very much. It was Mary Barry. She was bleeding from the neck. I got hold of her round the waist with my left arm, and tried to stop the blood with my right hand. I and another man took her into the house, and put her on the sofa. I said to her: 'Whoever has done this?'. She said: 'my husband has done it'. She never spoke afterwards; I remained with her until she died. This was about half an hour after. I then went upstairs where Wiliam Barry was. A policeman had hold of him on one side, and Edward Leach on the other. The prisoner had his head down and it was bleeding. He said nothing to me then. I remained there during the day. Barry during the day said: 'Its a very bad job'. I had known the prisoner about two years. He appeared to me to be quite sensible. He appeared all right that morning, he did not talk much at first. I never saw anything wrong to him while I have known him. We have had a glass together now and then. I never saw anything to lead me to judge that anything was wrong with him".

William Barry, a 35-year-old corn miller, was in the dock, accused of the Wilful Murder of his 33-year-old wife, Mary Barry, a mother of two, expecting for a third time. The couple had been staying at the Ormskirk Road home of Mary Barry's sister Kate Leach.

The deceased woman and the accused were said to have been on good terms and there seemed little motive for the heinous crime. There

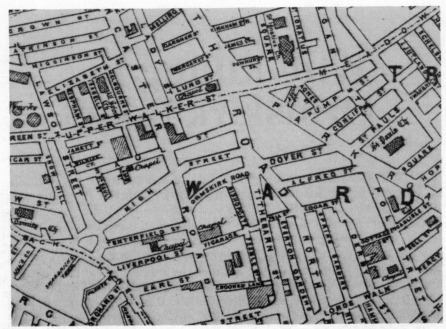

Henry Ashworth busily loading a cart in Bishopgate heard a terrifying scream in nearby Ormskirk Road

was little doubt that William Barry had inflicted the fatal wounds on his wife and then inflicted himself with the same weapon.

Details of the night of the crime were revealed to the jury by Catherine Leach who told a grim tale. She explained how, at about four o'clock in the morning, her sister had called out "Kate, Will can't sleep, the dogs keep running up and down the stairs". The sister then went out and put the dogs in the cupboard under the stairs. The gas lights were then lowered and the house went back to to rest until awoken by the chilling cry of "Oh! Kate". some ninety minutes later.

Immediately, Catherine Leach along with her husband, Edward, entered the sister's bedroom and discovered her mortally wounded in the throat. Alongside her was her husband, also wounded in the throat, and in his hand was a common pocket clasp knife which was covered in blood.

Being alerted by the cries of alarm, a police constable of the Borough, was soon at the house. With Henry Ashworth and others attending to the needs of the dying woman, he turned his attention to the perpetrator of the deed. In the upstairs room where the violence had occurred, Edward Leach was holding a firm grip on William Barry. The constable took the pocket knife, with its two inch long blade, from the prisoner and then attended to his self-inflicted wound.

With blood gushing from her jugular vein, the unfortunate woman's only relief was to be death itself, which came very quickly.

Evidence was presented in court to show that William Barry had been in low spirits and it was this aspect that the defence dwelled upon. His health was reported to have been generally poor and it was stated that he had talked about drowning himself.

Lengthy medical evidence was deliberated and opinion was sought as to whether or not the crime was committed due to homicidal mania. Surgeon, Mr. Spencer, was questioned about the state of the accused when he attended him on the morning after the killing. His conclusion was that at the time he saw nothing in Barry's behaviour to infer that he was insane.

This diagnosis led the defence to emphasise their claim that it was an impulse of homicidal mania. Mr. Spencer acknowledged that this could be the case and related that less than an hour after his examination of the accused it had taken four or five men to hold him as he displayed a violent rage.

When the defence counsel addressed the jury on behalf of the prisoner, he emphasised the lack of a motive for the crime and the confused state of the prisoner's mind. He stated the fact that the accused had made no attempt to choose a place to commit the crime where he could have concealed his action. He had at once tried to put an end to his own existence and when approached, firstly by his brother-in-law , and then by the police, had confessed that it was his hand that had taken away his wife's life.

At the end of a trial, which entailed great medical intensity, the Jury acquitted the prisoner on the grounds of insanity. Saved from the gallows, he was ordered to be detained during Her Majesty's Pleasure by Mr. Justice Mellor.

Postscript :

The following day, Stephen Burke, a Preston tailor, appeared in the same Crown Court room accused of the murder of his wife. Unlike William Barry he was found guilty of the capital offence and was hung on the last Saturday in March, 1865.

Tragedy at Deepdale Station

IN the early days of the Preston and Longridge Railway the motive power was supplied by means of horses. The carriages were drawn from Preston to the terminus at Longridge, by horses. On the return journey, owing to the downward gradient, the carriages ran by their own momentum to an area near Grimsargh Station and were afterwards horse-drawn to Preston. In connection with the Longridge line there were two stations at Preston, one in Deepdale Road and the other in Maudland Road. Both of them were of a very insignificant character, especially the latter, which consisted of nothing more than a narrow platform and a wooden, sentry-like box, from which the tickets were issued.

Steam was first used on this line in 1848. On 12th June of that year, a special inaugural train ran from Preston to Longridge and back. The engine was named "Addison" after Thomas Batty Addison, Esq., the chairman of the company and about 150 persons invited and accompanied by the directors, were in the train.

The railways were always of interest to the town's residents and spectators often visited the stations to watch the steam engines go by. The Deepdale Station of the Longridge Railway Company had its share of visitors. Often children would gather on the platform to await the arrival of a schedule train. Such an occasion was on Sunday 16th December, 1866. That afternoon a number of girls waited on the platform for the train from Longridge due at about three o'clock.

When the train arrived at Deepdale Station, a passenger named Henry Whittaker, a woolstapler, from Haslingden, saw a man smoking and held his hand out for a light. The train was stopped at the platform for about four minutes and the girls—about eight in total, had been dancing and chattering as it drew into the station.

70

As the train moved off, the girls walked along the side of the platform and it was there that tragedy struck. First one girl appeared to grab for Whittaker's outstretched hand and then another, who was 15-year-old Margaret Banks, the daughter of Mr. Thomas Banks, Secretary of the Spinners and Minders' Association. Whittaker's and the girl's hands were clutched together as the engine gained speed. Her friend, Mary Flynn, shouted "Maggie, Maggie, leave loose; but she did not free herself from Whittaker's grasp. The girl then appeared to twist round with her crinoline becoming hooked up to the carriage. She fell on her side, then slipped down between the platform and the wheels of the carriage and was killed instantly. The train passed over her head and also over one of her legs and arms. Immediately she was removed from the rails to the Station Tavern and a doctor was sent for. Her friends were in a state of great agitation and felt that the train passenger had been responsible for the tragedy, having held on to the teenager's hand for an instant too long.

When the Inquest was held on the Monday afternoon at the police station, the father of the deceased girl was present, as was the passenger on the train Henry Whittaker. The girl's friend, Mary Flynn, was the first witness called and she stated how her friend had struggled to get away from Whittaker, and had told the man: "Leave go", or something of that sort.

Rawstorne Whittaker, brother of Henry Whittaker, was in the same carriage and told the Inquest that he did not see his brother put his hand out, but had heard him asking for a light or a match. He was sat at the other side of the carriage and did not see what developed. When he heard the scream he thought his brother was sitting down in the carriage.

Henry Whittaker himself said the deceased got hold of his hand and she afterwards let go, how she got under the wheels he could not tell. He was also asked if when his hand was out of the carriage he had used the words: "Who'll have it". His response was that he never spoke a word to anyone.

The Coroner, in summing up, pointed out to the jury that the evidence was of a contradictory nature and said if Whittaker got hold of the deceased's hand and stuck to it, he would be guilty of manslaughter, but if the girl got hold of his hand and stuck to it, then he would not be answerable for her death.

The jury subsequently returned a verdict of "Accidental Death" and they then asked that some caution ought to be given to the railway company that they ought not to allow girls to go about playing on the station platform.

Mr. Walmsley, secretary of the Preston and Longridge Railway responded by saying that the booking office was on the platform; that the gates were closed until a short time before the trains arrived, that it was impossible to keep persons out of the station. Two out of three witnesses who gave evidence, he pointed out, had stated they went to the station for the purpose of going to Maudlands, and as the ticket office is on the platform we have no chance of preventing them from going there.

He continued by stating that the guard had distinctly told him that he had looked the length of the platform, and that everything was clear when he gave the signal to go on. If people will after that, when all the doors are locked, and when the signal to go on has been given,

On Sunday, December 16th, 1866 Police Constable John Bennett witnessed a tragic incident from his vantage point on the Deepdale Road bridge adjacent to the Deepdale Railway Station.

deliberately rush to the carriages, you cannot blame the Company for the consequences. The proceedings then terminated.

That was not the end of the matter, however, as in the first week of January, 1867, Henry Whittaker appeared in Preston Police Court charged with having caused the death of Margaret Banks, the 15-year-old power loom weaver. Once again the events of the tragic afternoon were related and varying accounts were given of the incident. Police Constable John Bennett told the court that on the Sunday afternoon he was on duty in Deepdale Road, and was standing on the bridge when the train came in. He said: "I saw the train stop and a man put his hand out of the carriage window. I saw some girls on the station, and one of them moved towards it and then Margaret Banks pushed her away and put her hand towards the hand that was out of the carriage window; I do not know which got hold. The train afterwards started and Margaret Banks was dragged about three yards and then she fell down between the train and the platform. I ran down to the platform and found the girl on the rails dead".

After the submissions of various witnesses who once again gave evidence of a contradictory character, the magistrates retired to consider their verdict. Ten minutes later they returned to inform Henry Whittaker that the evidence had been well weighed and considered and they felt it was not sufficient to commit him for trial. He was then discharged.

The Appalling End of Matthew Sansom

THE decade that began in 1840, was one of despair. Poverty and strife abounded among the working classes. Labour was at the mercy of capital, and though a man toiled from dawn to dusk he scarcely earned enough to pay the rent. Men, women and children grew visibly thinner, yet they worked like slaves. There was a great scarcity of food and it cast a gloom over the lives of young and old.

It was against this background that the events of the first Monday in November, 1849, unfolded. There was, at that time, living in the neighbourhood of Stonygate at 3 St. John's Place, the family of Matthew Sansom. The family consisted of husband and wife and seven children, and they found themselves in very low and straitened circumstances due to the fact that the husband had been unemployed for several months. He had previously been employed as a clerk in a solicitor's office and his failure to obtain another such situation preyed upon him and depressed his spirits.

Sometime on the Monday morning he had left his home, having, according to reports, eaten the last crust of bread in the house. He did not return home until after nine o'clock that night and when he did, he appeared as though he had drunk a glass or two of ale. He had eaten nothing that day and in consequence the liquor affected him more than usual. He rambled in his conversation, sometimes being quite kind and speaking sensibly and the next moment appearing quite excited and threatening. His wife Eliza, fearing that he intended some violence, left the house and went to the home of her next door neighbour Isabella Brooksby.

On the neighbour's advice, the wife of Matthew Sansom alerted a local constable, who returned to her home with her. His appearance calmed the husband down and the officer left with all appearing peaceful. No sooner had he gone than Matthew Sansom recommenced his threatening behaviour. As he went upstairs to where the children lay asleep, his wife Eliza, fearing for their safety, once again dashed to the neighbour's house.

Mrs. Brooksby, at the request of Eliza Sansom, went to the back door of the house and knocked. When Matthew Sansom appeared at the door he at first thought it was his wife and grabbed the woman. Releasing her, as soon as he realised his error, he called out: "What do you want?" To which the woman replied: "For you to let your wife and children go to bed".

Matthew Sansom's response was to beckon the woman inside, calling out: "Come in", in a very excited manner. As Mrs. Brooksby moved through the doorway, he reached onto the kitchen table with an outstretched arm and picked up an open razor. Then, as he uttered the words: "Well, then, here goes for it". He turned his shirt collar down with one hand, and drew the razor across his throat with the other. He then stood quite still watching the blood flowing from his neck.

Mrs. Brooksby was horror-struck and turned and ran up the yard screaming. Her piercing cries alerted the constable who was patrolling

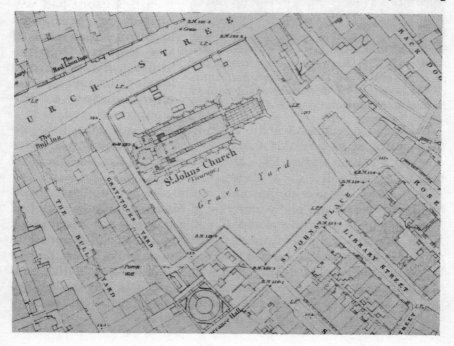

At number 3 St. John's Place situated opposite St. John's graveyard, lived Matthew Sansom in abject poverty. His desperate plight caused him to cut his own throat with a razor.

the area. At once he went to the house and there in the kitchen slumped in a corner was the unfortunate man.

Death occurred in less than five minutes due to the severance of the jugular vein. The blood gushed in such a stream that the floor was completely flooded with it. It was as if a bullock had been slaughtered. Indeed those who rushed inside the house to render assistance were obliged to wade through it.

Eliza Sansom had witnessed her husband's tragic act, having followed Mrs. Brooksby into the house yard and stood looking through the kitchen window as the drama developed.

The following morning, at the Town Hall, the inquest was held into the death of the 39-year-old father of seven. It was a sorry story that was recalled, and both his wife Eliza, and the neighbour, Mrs. Brooksby told their tragic tale.

The wife told the hearing that on several occasions lately her husband had been rather wild and wandering in his mind, and that she had frequently been afraid he would do some mischief to himself or his family. In consequence of wanting food, he had been very despondent and on occasions when he had taken a glass or two of liquor, he had been quite dangerous in his conduct, frequently talking of murders, and of his fear for his children. Among the ramblings and excited expressions which he made to his wife during the course of the evening was the phrase: "I will put us all out of our poverty".

Mrs. Brooksby also told of the strange behaviour of Matthew Sansom, particularly after he had partaken of drink, describing him as very wild and excited on those occasions.

As the inquest drew to a close the jury retired to consider their verdict, and when they returned they announced the following decision: "Matthew Sansom cut his throat with a razor whilst labouring under temporary insanity". For the unfortunate man the struggle had been too great to bear after a decade when famine had been a reality for the family of Matthew Sansom.

Trouble at the Rosebud

ON the last Monday in June, 1857, Matthew Tyson, a fishmonger, and his wife, Mary, attended a wedding party at the Three Crowns beerhouse in Stanley Street, Preston. By half past three in the afternoon the wedding guests were beginning to disperse and the Tysons decided to make their way to the Rosebud public house, at the top of Stanley Street, on the New Hall Lane and London Road junction.

What they saw, as they walked from one beerhouse to the other, was to result in Mary Tyson appearing before Miles Myres, the coroner, at the Inquest into the death of Owen McCullock a tailor, who had resided in Hoghton Square.

The fishmonger's wife addressed the Inquest with the following words:

"On our way to the Rosebud we met Owen McCullock running to get out of the way of some men. He was accompanied by John Procter. There were four or five navvies after them, one of whom struck Procter, who then ran into the Three Crowns by the back way. Procter left McCullock amongst the crowd outside the public house. One of the navvies addressing McCullock said: "I will give you as much as Procter has got". I don't know the person who said so. Then Robert Wilkinson said to McCullock: "I can fight you, and give you as much as will satisfy you".

He then pushed at McCullock, who, in return, struck him. A fight then took place. During the fight, I saw Wilkinson kick McCullock twice on the bottom part of the belly. McCullock immediately fell upon the ground. Wilkinson looked at McCullock about a minute, and then went into the crowd. McCullock was then lifted up and carried into the Three Crowns, where he was laid upon a sofa. He seemed insensible and was unable to walk".

Mary McCullock, the wife of Owen McCullock, told the hearing that her 43-year-old husband had died on Sunday, July 5th, six days after the fatal fight in Stanley Street. She had not seen him that night when he arrived home hurt, but saw him in bed just before noon on the Tuesday. He complained of being unwell, and said: "I am killed".

Local surgeon Lawrence Spencer was called in to attend him and he continually treated him until his death. He told the Inquest that he was convinced that Owen McCullock died from the effects of the injuries he received on the day in question. Such injuries could readily be produced by a kick.

William Barton, a local police constable, told the Inquest that he had apprehended Robert Wilkinson on the Thursday before McCullock's death. Wilkinson telling him: "I am very sorry, it is the first time I have been in your hands. Is there no way of making it up between our two selves".

He then told the Inquest that he had taken Wilkinson to the police station and then to McCullock's home in Hoghton Square, where the following conversation took place:

McCullock said: "That's the man that kicked me".

Wilkinson replying: "You struck me first".

McCullock responding: "I never did".

Wilkinson remarking: "I am very sorry, can we not make it up betwixt our two selves".

McCullock then shook his head, and said: "You have killed me".

Wilkinson was then taken back to the police station.

In an attempt to unravel the reason for the fight, James Parkinson, the son of the landlord of The Rosebud, was called. He told the hearing that earlier in the afternoon there had been a disturbance in The Rosebud. Wilkinson and some other men had been in the front parlour of the public house and had followed Procter and McCullock into the kitchen. Procter was seen by the witness holding a man upon the floor, knocking his head upon the stone flags.

When the coroner summed up he said the question they had to determine was whether the prisoner, Robert Wilkinson, had kicked the deceased or not. If they were perfectly satisfied that his death had not been caused by the injuries that resulted, then it was clear that the prisoner was not guilty of manslaughter. He reminded the jury that a man was justified only in using his fists in self defence, and that it was illegal for him to use his feet.

The Rosebud Inn, New Hall Lane, as it appeared in the early years of this century. A disturbance at the Rosebud Inn, on a Monday in June, 1857, led to a fatal fight in Stanley Street.

After a brief deliberation, the jury returned with the following verdict: "We find the death of Owen McCullock to have been caused from injuries inflicted upon him by Robert Wilkinson, the prisoner. The coroner then asked "Then you record a verdict of manslaughter against Robert Wilkinson. To which the foreman of the jury replied "We do".

Robert Wilkinson, who was present during the inquiry, seemed much affected on hearing the decision of the jury.

Subsequently Wilkinson, who was employed upon the sewage works, in course of construction in Avenham Lane, was taken into custody to await his trial at Lancaster Assizes.

Within weeks he appeared in the Crown Court and the details of the June afternoon were again related. The jury, before they retired, were given the following advice by His Lordship: "It does not matter who provoked the fight; so long as a fight ensued, and one was killed, the survivor was guilty of the crime of manslaughter. If a fight ensued — no matter how fair the fight might be — and death resulted, it was manslaughter.

He then told the jury that it was up to them to say whether the prisoner had been simply defending himself from an assault or been engaged in a fight.

The jury were absent for half-an-hour and when they returned they brought in a verdict of "Guilty" with a recommendation to mercy, on the grounds of his good character and the provocation he had received from McCullock.

It was a couple of days before sentence was passed on Robert Wilkinson and when it was, it was that he should be imprisoned for two calendar months.

Pandemonium in Preston Gaol

EARLY in January, 1858, a 59-year-old man Robert Kershaw, suffered a violent death at Over Darwen and as a result one of his sons Thomas Kershaw, a 19-year-old steam-loom weaver was subseqently committed for trial at Lancaster Assizes accused of his murder. Upon his committal he was transferred to the House of Correction at Preston, to await the forthcoming sessions.

Upon his arrival in Preston, Thomas Kershaw was placed in one of the hospital wards of the Preston Gaol with two orderlies in constant attendance upon him, due to his irrational behaviour. His appearance caused uneasiness in the hospital cell block and finally on the morning of 12th February, before dawn broke, the situation erupted. Sleeping in the next bed to him was Charles Collins, one of those entrusted with the task of watching Kershaw. Suddenly without warning Kershaw leapt from his bed and grabbing a heavy fire shovel from the grate made towards the bed that Collins occupied. Then with all the ferocity of a madman, he rained some half a dozen blows to the head of the unaware Collins. Pandemonium followed and awoken by the noise of the affair another inmate Richard Gornall sprang from his bed and grappled with Kershaw. He succeeded in overpowering him and in wrestling the weapon from his grasp.

Hell bent on destruction, Kershaw then lunged his hand through one of the cell windows, seizing one of the bars on the outside he gripped it as though he could wrench it from the fastenings and escape. Finding he could not accomplish this, he lay down on his bed again, and did not show any further signs of violence.

The Governor, Colonel Martin and Mr. Dixon the gaol surgeon, were sent for immediately and when they arrived they found Collins groaning on the bed with his head and face and a large portion of the flooring of the room covered with blood. The distraught victim was suffering from five scalp wounds of a serious nature. He was immediately given a measure of brandy and his wounds were dressed.

It appeared that Kershaw had rambled strangely since his incarceration and to the other inmates had admitted that he had murdered his father by striking him on the head with a poker. While still alive, he had dragged him into the cellar, and that he intended to lay all the blame for the killing on his mother, who he claimed was insane and he would, therefore be acquitted.

Apparently Collins, who was serving a sentence for obtaining goods by false pretences had been a witness to all the ramblings of Kershaw, and repenting of the confidence he had placed in Collins his action was an attempt to silence him, less his testimony should be a damaging indictment at his trial.

While the Governor was attending to Collins, Kershaw lying on his own bed called out: "I'm bleeding to death—look here", showing his right hand, which was slightly cut by the glass he had broken in the window. A strait jacket was immediately placed upon him and he was placed under the strictest of supervision.

The following day an examination took place in the hospital ward before the visiting justices. The charge attributed to Kershaw was one of attempting to murder one of the hospital orderlies. Collins, who was confined to his bed and was in a pitiable state, was the first to be examined and explained how he had been knocked insensible by the ferocious attack. The magistrates were shown the shovel and force of the blows was reflected in the fact that one side of the shovel had been bent under the onslaught. He was, despite his condition, able to relate how Kershaw had made threats to him during the week and had remarked "I may as well be hung for two murders as for one".

Other inmates of the gaol testified as to Kershaws actions that night and his general threatening behaviour and it was finally concluded that the attempted murder charge be added to his other indictment.

Two weeks later the focus of attention was the Crown Court, Lancaster where Mr. Baron Martin presided over the Assizes. In the dock stood Kershaw and alongside him was his mother. Kershaw faced a charge of wounding one Charles Collins with intent to murder him besides the indictment for his father's death. His 53-year-old mother, Catherine Kershaw, was accused of harbouring, receiving and maintaining her son, knowing him to have committed the killing of her husband.

Robert an elder brother of Kershaw's, told how his brother had informed him of the killing and the concealment of his father in the cellar. On arriving home that day he had been told that his father had gone out for the evening and only when he went to bed with his brother was he told the terrible tale.

The accused had suggested that the brothers go together to Liverpool that night and board a ship for some foreign part. Stunned by his brother's revelations, Robert Kershaw made his way to the cellar with a lighted candle and searched through the coals, eventually discovering a naked leg underneath the pile of fuel.

He immediately left the house and went to his uncle's house, and as a result the police were sent for and the shocking tragedy revealed to all.

The father had been in failing health for sometime and been something of a burden on the family. Husband and wife had lived together far from harmoniously, and Thomas Kershaw had been at loggerheads with his father. That fateful day the situation became intolerable in the mind of the accused and he dealt his father a killing blow.

Once all the testimony had been delivered, His Lordship observed that there was no evidence against the widow of the deceased, and directed the jury to find her innocent.

Concerning Thomas Kershaw there was little doubt as to his action but the dilemma facing the jury was whether his actions had been those of a sane man.

At the beginning of the proceedings, when asked how he pleaded, he had admitted the crime at Preston Gaol but uttered his innocence over the charge of killing his father. The jury had only a brief consultation and when they had finished they informed His Lordship that their verdict was "Not Guilty upon the ground of insanity".

The Preston crime was taken as confirmation of his insanity and it was eminently obvious remarked Baron Martin that Kershaw must be prevented from doing such acts in the future. Consequently he announced that Thomas Kershaw be imprisoned during Her Majesty's Pleasure. He was then removed from the dock to return to his incarceration.

Throughout the trial he had stood listlessly, either with his eyes closed or looking vacantly around, appearing to take no interest in the proceedings.

When Cholera Came to Town

IN 1832, the dreaded Cholera ravaged towns and cities throughout the land. Particularly hit were the northern towns of Warrington and Wigan.

The bilious disease marked by purging, vomiting and griping pains struck with uncompassionate ferocity. In its wake it left great fear, which aroused the consciousness of the people to the need for better sanitary conditions. Considerable strides were made in that direction, although standards of hygiene still left a lot to be desired.

Whilst the Cholera was taking its toll nearby, providence smiled upon the people of Preston, for it chose not to visit the town that year.

Sixteen years later when the dreaded disease was again in the public's consciousness a great deal of apprehension was felt.

The fear led one anxious and concerned resident of Preston to pen a letter for publication in the *Preston Guardian*. It was his second contribution to the columns inside two weeks. It warned of the dreaded cholera and it read as follows:

> "Sir,
> A fortnight ago I drew attention, through the means of your journal, to the filthy state of our public streets, Fishergate and Church Street, and to the accumulation of dirt and refuse of all sorts in the channels of these streets. I had hoped that these nuisances might before this have been removed, but such is not the case.
> I said then that cholera was approaching, it is now actually in our kingdom, cases have occurred and still continue daily; and who knows how soon the fatal malady may visit our town, and carry off some of its worthiest inhabitants.

James Holden, a 48-year-old glazier, was 'siezed' of the Cholera at 2 o'clock in the morning in late July, 1848. He died before noon of the same day

Let us put on our armour and be prepared. Let our public bodies, one and all, exert themselves nobly to oppose the entrance of the formidable invader now so near us.

It needs no acuteness of smell or sight to prove that our town is not as cleanly as it might, and ought to be. Hundreds are unemployed; could not some of these be engaged to act in cleansing and purifying? I think so; and hope these remarks offend no one, but merely excite investigation.

I remain, yours Salos"

By August the words of warning had become all too true, as the *Preston Guardian* began to weekly record, several fatal cases in the town and neighbourhood.

The alarm was raised following the death on a Thursday morning in late July of James Holden. He was a 48-year-old glazier, who resided in a cellar at 9 Vicar Street. He was 'seized' at two o'clock in the morning and died just before noon that day.

A surgeon from the Dispensary attended upon him and reported that he had found the premises in an abominable state of filth.

The victims body was interred as soon as the Inspector of Nuisances was informed and the premises were subjected to a cleaning and whitewashing.

Cholera Morbus.

To the Inhabitants of Preston generally.

AT a time like the present, when a pestilential disease is prevailing throughout the Country, and when most of the towns in this neighbourhood are suffering more or less from its ravages, it is a subject of no small interest to every Inhabitant of Preston and its Neighbourhood, how he may ward off the attack of this remorseless Distemper, and how, if attacked, he may abate its violence.

With a view to render as much assistance as lies within the sphere of my small ability, to those who are willing to be guided by my advice on this awful occasion, I am prompted to the present undertaking, in which I propose to recommend the adoption of a few Rules that have appeared to me likely to be subservient to the object I have in view, namely, the welfare and happiness of my fellow townsmen. I therefore advise

1st.—That the Inhabitants of Preston entirely abstain from eating Fruit of all kinds, and such Vegetables as are flatulent and the most liable to fermentation, as Cabbage, Pease, Cauliflower, and Cucumber. That Potatoes when used, be well boiled, and quite freed from the water in which they were boiled, and that Salt be freely used with the food.

2ndly.—That every Individual, whether rich or poor, be rigidly abstemious in eating and drinking, and that he totally avoid the use of Ale and Porter, both of which at this season of the year are exceedingly unwholesome.

3rdly.—That in order to ensure perfect Cleanliness of person, every Inhabitant of the town and its neighbourhood daily sponge or wash his whole body with water, beginning with a moderately warm temperature, and gradually decreasing it to cold; and that in addition to a flannel shirt, he wear a broad flannel belt round his waist, so as completely to cover his bowels.

4thly.—That on feeling the slightest derangement of the Stomach or Bowels, the Invalid, if an adult, take two table-spoons full of Castor Oil, thirty Drops of Laudanum, and thirty of Æther, in a wineglass full of strong Peppermint-water, sipping frequently of strong Brandy and water, and that Medical aid be called in as early as possible.

5thly.—That all Yards, Channels, and Privies, be kept perfectly clean ; that all offensive matter, or matter liable to become offensive, be instantly removed from the dwelling, and the vehicle thoroughly washed ; and that the Rooms of every house be well ventilated.

6thly.—That on the slightest appearance of Choleretic symptoms in the family, the floors of the house, more especially around the bed of the patient, be freely sprinkled with solution of Chloride of Lime.

By observing the above Rules, the writer of this address is led to believe, that, if the scourge which we have all so much reason to dread be not entirely averted, it may at least be moderated; but he would build his hopes of preservation not on human means and human aid, but on the ALMIGHTY, who only is able to deliver us from this noisome pestilence.

AMICUS.

JULY 26TH, 1832.

Pritt, Printer, 29, Fishergate, Preston.

An 1832 poster "to the inhabitants of Preston generally" warning of the dangers of the dreaded scourge of Cholera Morbus. Remarkably, Preston escaped the 1832 Cholera visitation.

Cholera — The Fearsome Disease

Cholera is a fearsome disease which, untreated, is lethal in a high percentage of its victims; it is caused by a micro-organism — the Cholera Vibrio which attacks the lining of the gut and causes it to break down. When it does, large quantities of fluid are poured forth and it is the consequent dehydration, with loss of electrolytes (the mineral contents of the blood), which usually kill the victim. Healthy individuals are largely immune, because the normal stomach acid kills off the invader before it can kill the host.

Today we have several weapons in our armoury to deal with this disease. Those at risk can be immunised. When already infected, the individual can be treated with potent antibiotics, or if the disease has become established, dehydration can be dealt with by giving intravenous saline. But in the early 19th century none of this was known or available.

It was not until 1849, that it became known that drinking water was the main source of infection.

The same day's newspaper carried details of a recipe of medicine to be kept at hand in case of cholera and to be taken until proper medical aid could be obtained —

"Confection of opium, $1\frac{1}{2}$ drams; aromatic confection, 2 drams; compund tincture of cinnamon, $\frac{1}{4}$ ounce; tincture of opium, 60 drops; chalk mixture, $7\frac{1}{2}$ ounces; three table spoonfuls to be taken every half hour while the pain continues".

Some five weeks later the paper announced another case of cholera in Vicar Street. This time it was No.11 — once again it was a resident of a cellar. The man was Theo. Dagger, a 35-year-old labourer. He was 'seized' about seven o'clock in the morning and passed away shortly after six the same evening. By mid morning he had been attended by the local surgeon, but his efforts had been to no avail.

The corpse was interred the following morning and to the surgeon's instructions his bed was to be removed, and along with the bedding and clothes it was committed to flames.

Cases of cholera were now beginning to be reported in various neighbourhoods. A year later, in August, 1849, the town's attention focused on Bleasdale Street, off Ribbleton Lane. In one week three deaths were reported from that street, a 49-year-old woman who lived at No. 15, and a woman and her four-year-old child, who occupied No. 2 Bleasdale Street. The Inspector of Nuisances was immediately alerted and he was scathing in his criticism of the area. The street was in a disgraceful state, with an exposed and open sewer, filth lying up and down, noxious and offensive smells all combining to render the place "the chosen abode of pestilence and death".

Elsewhere that week two adult males and a four-year-old girl fell victims to the dreaded disease.

The *Preston Guardian* described the cholera as a health inspector that speaks in a language no man can misunderstand. It visits, the reader was reminded, the neglected lunatic in his cell, the crowded workhouse, the homes of pauper children, the undrained city, the uncleaned street, the cellar and the attic. The conclusion was that it was the penalty of man's own negligence and indiscretion. Filthy persons, inhabiting filthy houses, in filthy neighbourhoods, and addicted to intemperate habits being the main victims of the visitation.

Poison Purchased in Church Street

AT Christmas, 1854, the marriage took place of Ellen Holden, the daughter of a hand-loom weaver, with Edward Hardman, a shoe-maker, from Chorley. The couple set up home at Brindle, but did not stay there quite twelve months, their union being not entirely a happy one. The fact that they were of different religious creeds, Edward Hardman being a Roman Catholic, and his wife a member of the Church of England, did not help to create harmony. This and other sources of difference producing a separation with Ellen Hardman returning to her parents home.

She stayed with her parents about three months before resuming her marriage by going to live with her husband in the area known as Botany Bay—about one mile from Chorley. She had responded to her husband's plea, and the second period of their wedded life seemed much better and did not appear to produce the differences that had led to their separation. One condition she agreed to in October, 1856, when she bore his child was that the infant would be brought up in his faith.

After her confinement, she appeared to be in good health and therefore her father, William Holden, was surprised in February, 1857, when he received a letter from his son-in-law, informing him that his daughter had been taken ill.

The next morning, Thursday, 26th February, he went over to his daughter's home and found her in a low state of weakness. She said she had been taken ill after having some broth, and that it had such an effect on her that she thought she was going to die that instant. Her father stayed with her about three hours and gave her some toast and water. She had been vomiting in the morning but when he left she seemed a little better.

On the following Sunday, he received another note from his son-in-law, and again visited his daughter, who appeared not to have changed much in her sickness. She complained of vomiting in the morning and had little appetite for any food although her father managed to feed her with a little gruel.

On the Monday morning, Edward Hardman, who to all accounts had treated his wife well during her illness, told her he was going to visit Preston to settle an outstanding account with a leather seller and furrier in the town. Once in Preston he met up with John Ashburner, another shoemaker from Chorley, and asked him if he would accompany him to a druggists shop. The pair then going to 26 Church Street, Preston, the shop of Henry Critchley. Hardman asking for a half-a-pound of arsenic, which he stated was to rid his home of bugs. The chemist as was his duty asked Hardman for a reference and he quoted the name of a common acquaintance. Both Hardman and Ashburner then signed the druggist's record book as requested, but Hardman stated his address was Bamber Bridge. Henry Critchley, in line with an Act of Parliament, mixed half-an-ounce of blue (indigo) colouring matter with the arsenic poison before he handed the package to Edward Hardman.

On the Monday night, Ellen Hardman seemed a little better and got up to her tea. On the Tuesday she was up again, but not long, and on the Wednesday she was taken 'very badly' in the early evening. Her father was summoned to the house and he found her in a worse state than he had ever seen her. Thursday dawned with no improvement, as the day wore on she was extremely purged and vomited; she became much exhausted and gradually got worse and worse until she died. She appeared black under the eyes, she had a dewy, clammy skin, aching of the limbs and was blue and cold at the extremities.

Dr. Smith the medical attendant, attributed her death to gastro-enteritis and inflammation of the bowels.

With the husband and child in mourning the woman was buried within days. It was a respectable funeral with several people there and after the interment Hardman provided beef and ale at a local public house.

Following the funeral, remarks prejudicial to Hardman began to be made and having heard the rumours, he appeared at the police station to protest at them. However enquires had already been instituted and eleven days after the burial, Mrs. Hardman's body was exhumed. The subsequent post-mortem examination revealed traces of antimony, an unquestionable poison, and also slight traces of arsenic. The conclusion was drawn that the woman had met her death as a result of poisoning. Edward Hardman was at once taken into custody at Preston's House of Correction.

Investigations later revealed that he had been to Preston to purchase the arsenic and that earlier in February, he had purchased a drachm of 60 grains of tartar emetic (a form of tartarized antimony) from a chemist in Chorley.

At the beginning of August, 1857, Edward Hardman, aged 28, appeared in the Crown Court of Lancaster Assizes, charged with the Wilful Murder of his wife.

Once proceedings were in full swing the crowded court heard how Mrs. Hardman had been taken ill on Shrove Tuesday, 1857, and had eventually died during the following week. Midway through his wife's illness, the accused had uttered conflicting reports, firstly telling the attendant doctor his wife was on the road to recovery and then informing her father, through a messenger, that she was about to breath her last.

Numerous witnesses verified that the prisoner had possession of the poisons and spoke of his administering curiously tasting mixtures to his wife during the days of her illness.

The court was also told how the accused had, within days of his wife's death, been in contact with another woman. He had apparently sent a message to a woman by the name of Sherrington, asking her to come and see him, and telling her: "She had nothing to do but come and hang her bonnet up in his house".

Another witness recalled that when she enquired on the day of Ellen Hardman's death as to her condition and offered the suggestion, that she may have typhus fever, Hardman had replied: "Typhus fever be buggered, I know better than that".

When His Lordship began his summing up of the case he went over the medical evidence and the undeniable conclusion was that the woman had been poisoned. He then proceeded to go over the other evidence which pointed to the likelihood of the prisoner administering the poison.

The Jury were then locked away to consider their verdict. Among those charged with the task were an innkeeper and a grocer from Padiham, a tea dealer and a brazier from Lancaster, and a builder and draper from Preston. This collection of everyday honest folk took just 20 minutes to come to the conclusion that Edward Hardman was "Guilty as charged".

Late 19th century Church Street, Preston. One Monday morning in March, 1857, Edward Hardman visited a Church Street druggist to buy half-a-pound of arsenic

His Lordship then donned the black cap and proceeded to pass sentence of death on the accused, closing with the words: "May the Lord have mercy on your soul". The prisoner turned very pale and appeared to be trembling as he was removed from the dock.

The execution of Edward Hardman took place at precisely twelve o'clock on 29th August, 1857. A great number of people actually walked from Chorley and other towns and villages in East Lancashire to witness the public hanging. While each train that arrived at the county town was crowded with those eager to witness the end of the notorious shoemaker.

The hangman on this occasion was the experienced Calcraft, who had arrived the previous afternoon to prepare for his duty. Hardman was particularly anxious that the hangman should not obtain possession of his clothes, and the night before his execution he allotted the several articles of his apparel amongst the officers of the gaol.

Although he did not make a formal confession he was said to have replied: "None whatsoever", when asked if he had any fault to find with either the verdict of the Jury, or the sentence passed upon him.

When Hardman appeared on the scaffold his face was ashen pale and his lips continually moved in prayer. He was dressed in a decent-looking suit of black, which appeared to be little worn. In a moment the bolt was drawn, the trap fell and amid groans of pity from the large assembly the murderer ceased to exist.

An Incorrigible Offender

ON Whit Tuesday, 25th May, 1858, James Simpson and his wife, who ran a small provisions shop at 12 Deepdale Street, where in an upstairs room attending to a sick child when their attention was drawn to the cries of one of their daughters, a three-year-old infant. Her words were "Mammy, there has a man been and taken all the half-pennies". Her father immediately descended the stairs and ran out of the shop and was just in time to see a man, small in stature, making his hurried way into Deepdale Road and past Stephenson Terrace. He followed him for a while, but when the fugitive turned down Peel Hall Street he lost sight of him.

Unknown to the shopkeeper the man made his escape by passing through a stone yard in Peel Hall Street. An elderly couple who kept watch on the stone yard shouted to the man that there was no road through; he ignored their remarks and hurried on his way.

The couple were able to describe the man sufficiently for the local police to be on the look-out and on the following Thursday morning, Police Constable Stirzaker saw a man in the street who answered to the description. As the constable approached him however, the suspect bolted, escaping through a yard and over a set of railings nine feet high. Later that morning the determined officer traced him to his lodgings in Stanley Street, where he made his arrest. Once he had him handcuffed, the constable informed him that he was arresting him for robbing a till on Whit Tuesday. The prisoner responded by saying: "Oh, I'm alright, nobody see'd me", and then without warning he lurched towards the officer with his head, butting him in the belly. For a while the two men were locked in a struggle on the floor before the officer managed to regain the upper hand and led his prisoner off to the police station.

Stephenson Terrace, Preston, as it is today. After helping himself to three shillings from a shop till in Deepdale Street the fugitive fled past Stephenson Terrace and up to Peel Hall Street.

As a result the following morning Thomas Brown, a "diminutive wry fellow in his early twenties appeared before the magistrates. His stay in the lock-up at the police station had been an eventful one, as the gathering was about to discover.

Firstly the court dealt with the matter over which the suspect was arrested, which was the stealing of about three shillings, in silver and copper, from the till of the Deepdale Street shop.

The couple from the stone yard made a positive identification of Brown, and P.C. Stirzaker told of his ordeal in apprehending the accused. In response the prisoner pleaded guilty, and begged the mercy of the Bench saying he was very, very sorry for what he had done.

At this stage a second charge was brought against the accused, this being one of committing a ferocious attack on P.S. Leach, the night-sergeant at the police station. The officer appeared in court with a dreadfully swollen face, his left cheek being covered with a multiplicity of plasters.

For the next hour the magistrates were told of the incidents the previous night. It had begun around 6.30 p.m. when P.S. Leach had gone to visit Brown in his cell. On entering the room he had been assaulted by the prisoner who sprang at him, striking several blows to his face with a weapon, which he held in his hand. P.S. Leach was so confused by the sudden and violent nature of the attack that the villain overpowered him and escaped from the cell, making his way along the corridor and down a flight of stone steps into the cellar.

Despite his injuries the sergeant soon came to his senses and raised the alarm. Another constable alerted to the escape bid dashed out into the street to see Brown about to emerge from the coal-hole having removed the cellar grate. The officer's appearance caused the prisoner to retreat back into the cellar and as he did so another constable was on hand to apprehend him.

A close examination of the cell showed that the weapon used by Brown was a holdfast, which he had removed from around a water pipe in the closet. He had partially straightened the semi-circular clip and an inspection of the cell wall showed that he had been attempting to use this implement to make his escape through a thick brick wall. A hole about fifteen inches long, three inches deep and seven or eight broad, bore evidence to the industry with which he had worked since his incarceration.

That same night Supt. Gibbons, on visiting the prisoner in his fresh cell, saw him jump down from the window, and found that he had removed two squares of glass and had been busy on a third pane. From the feat, the prisoner had performed in his first cell, and the ingenuity he displayed there, it seemed that he would have soon found some means of removing the iron bars from the window and been bidding his gaolers 'goodbye'.

Mr. Gibbons consequently thought it prudent to take extraordinary precautions for the detention of Brown and he ordered him to be conveyed to a cell in the upper storey of the lock-up, where he was handcuffed and chained to an iron bar.

Despite all the precautions Brown was almost successful in securing his freedom the following morning, just hours before his appearance in court. One of the duty constables was assigned the task of taking the prisoner to wash himself. As his handcuffs were being removed, Brown diverted the constable's attention to the filthy state of the water closet. Within a flash the prisoner was past him and onto the corridor, with the cell door slamming behind him.

At once he made his way downstairs and towards the door of the station where he was confronted by two more officers. Once again he displayed his slipperiness and agility and only after a protracted struggle did one of the constables manage to collar him.

The magistrates took a dim view of the assault on the sergeant and they informed Brown that he must be committed to Lancaster for trial. For the robbery from the till he was given a sentence of three months hard labour. On hearing the sentence a woman, who passed as his wife, began crying loudly and muttering something that was unintelligible. On being remonstrated with by an officer, she became very violent and had to be forcibly removed by several officers. Brown himself was in a rage at the other end of the court and for about five minutes the whole place was in a complete uproar.

Ultimately at the beginning of August, 1858, Thomas Brown, collier, appeared at Lancaster Summer Assizes before His Lordship, Chief Baron Pollock. Accused of a murderous assault on a police officer which had left the sergeant with two deep wounds on his left cheek and a damaged jaw.

The prisoner cross-examined several witnesses with the tact of an Old Bailey practitioner, but was unable to shake their testimony. In his defence he claimed that P.S. Leach had caught his foot against something and had fallen with his face against the bed-board. Medical witnesses however testified that the injuries were not consistent with such an incident and the jury found him guilty of intent to do grevious bodily harm and also of resisting his lawful detainer.

When asked if he had anything to say before sentence was passed he simply stated that he was very sorry, that he had no parents to look after him, that he had a wife to whom he had been wed just a short time and he pleaded for mercy and the shortest possible sentence.

His Lordship stressed that resistance of the lawful authority was a "species of rebellion, that the police were appointed to preserve peace and order and that the man who resisted them deserved the heaviest punishment of the Law". He then informed Brown that his sentence was one of Ten Years Penal Servitude.

Immediately after he had received his sentence the prisoner was conveyed by the underground route into one of the range of 'silent system cells' branching from the Round-house. One of the warders later took him his dinner, closing the cell door as he left. However the spring lock on the door did not secure it properly and Brown was suddenly left with an unexpected opportunity to take his freedom, which he lost no time in taking advantage of.

The cell opened into a small exercise yard surrounded by an eleven foot high wall topped with sharpened stakes. In one corner of the yard was a water closet and by its help he succeeded in scaling the wall and palisading, dropping down into a small garden railed off from the old debtors' yard.

Having succeeded in reaching that point without observation, the most difficult aspect of his escape remained to be accomplished. It was necessary for him to present himself at the gateway, and pass the scrutiny of the turnkey who had admitted him the previous day.

Some visitors who had been looking through the castle were approaching the gate as he descended into the debtors' yard and he immediately tagged onto the rear. He was aware that a party of masons were working in the castle and with his coat under his arm he hoped to pass off as one of their number.

When between the gates, his appearance attracted the attention of Thomas Pennington, an old turnkey of the castle who enquired: "Well my lad, where art thou going?" With remarkable readiness he answered: "Oh, I am going for some tools", and in reply to a further question, coolly said: "the tools are for the masons".

So well did he play his part, that the gate was at once opened and he passed through without another word by Pennington. Walking at a quick pace he went down Castle Hill, Market Street, by the Kings Arms corner and onto the road for Preston.

It was supposed that Brown obtained his liberty about half past one o'clock that Tuesday afternoon and it was another hour before his escape was discovered.

An immediate search of Lancaster was started and telegrams were sent to Preston and to the headquarters of several county divisions. On receipt of the telegram, Supt. Gibbons of the Preston Borough Police Force issued the following notice which appeared in the *Preston Chronicle* week ending 14th August, 1858:

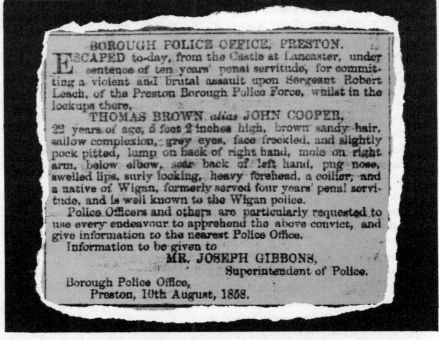

BOROUGH POLICE OFFICE, PRESTON.

ESCAPED to-day, from the Castle at Lancaster, under sentence of ten years' penal servitude, for committing a violent and brutal assault upon Sergeant Robert Leach, of the Preston Borough Police Force, whilst in the lockups there.

THOMAS BROWN. *alias* JOHN COOPER,

22 years of age, 5 feet 2 inches high, brown sandy hair, sallow complexion, grey eyes, face freckled, and slightly pock pitted, lump on back of right hand, mole on right arm, below elbow, scar back of left hand, pug nose, swelled lips, surly looking, heavy forehead, a collier, and a native of Wigan, formerly served four years' penal servitude, and is well known to the Wigan police.

Police Officers and others are particularly requested to use every endeavour to apprehend the above convict, and give information to the nearest Police Office.

Information to be given to

MR. JOSEPH GIBBONS,
Superintendent of Police.

Borough Police Office,
Preston, 10th August, 1858.

Meanwhile the search for Brown was intensifying as news was obtained that he had passed through Scotforth about three o' clock enquiring the road for Preston. Constables despatched from Preston met up with others from Lancaster and the net was beginning to close. It seemed that Brown's destination was Preston and the Garstang area became the focal point of the search.

Eventually the escaped convict was spotted by a constable in plain clothes as he made his way towards Myerscough. Suspicious of the approaching officer's scrutiny of him, Brown jumped over a hedge and alighted in a ditch. The constable likewise vaulted the hedge and soon the two men were locked in a struggle. Eventually the constable from the Lancaster borough overpowered his captive and took him to the Bowgrave lock-up.

From there he was returned to the Castle where he was placed in irons for safe custody.

By now there was great public interest in this determined gaol breaker and the young ruffian's criminal record added to the fascination. He had originated from the Wigan area and had a string of offences behind him. His speciality had been robbing tills and from 1849 to 1854 he was given several terms of imprisonment ranging from three months to four years for a till robbery in February 1854. After that term of incarceration he was reputed to have told the Chief Constable of Wigan that 'the penal settlements were dreadful and that he had every intention to be "a good lad". The day after that conversation he was before the magistrates again on a charge of picking pockets just fifty yards from the police station door. The magistrates considered him "incorrigible" and as he promised to amend his behaviour, they dismissed him; hearing no more from him till his exploits at Preston and his escape from Lancaster Castle.

Jane Parker "Kept to Hard Labour"

S HORTLY before noon on Saturday, 6th March, 1858, a woman appeared at the house of Mary Eaves in Ormskirk Road, Preston, and asked if she could be accommodated with lodgings during her imminent confinement. Mrs. Eaves acceded to her wishes and the woman was taken in.

She was taken ill a couple of hours later, and on the Sunday afternoon when in the pains of parturition, she expressed a desire to be delivered without surgical assistance. Mrs. Eaves would not listen to her plea and sent her daughter Elizabeth to fetch a Mr. Satterthwaite. With the medical man's assistance, the woman was delivered of a fine , healthy male child at a quarter-past-seven the same evening.

On Monday, the woman left her bed, and on Tuesday, about half-past-twelve o'clock, she took leave of Mrs. Eaves, saying she wished to attend to the duties of her situation. Stating that the old gentleman and lady with whom she lived kept a large farm and she was sole manager. The woman left the lodging house wearing a black cloth mantle, trimmed with broad black braid and a white straw bonnet. In her arms, she carried the newly-born infant which was clothed in garments made by the daughter of Mrs. Eaves.

Within a few minutes the woman was in the Black-a-Moors Head public house in Lancaster Road, ordering a gin and water and proudly showing her child to the landlady, informing her that it was less than two days old.

A little after one o'clock the woman appeared in Friargate at the premises of furniture broker John Westhead. She told him that she wished to purchase a small travelling box and requested that he tie a

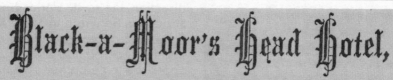

A 19th century advertisement for the Black-a-Moor's Hotel and photo as it appears today. At lunchtime on Tuesday, 9th March, 1858, a woman appeared at the Black-a-Moor's Head public house in Lancaster Road, she ordered a gin and water and proudly showed the landlady her newly-born child.

Friargate in the middle of the 19th century. The woman appeared in Friargate at the premises of furniture broker, John Westhead.

direction tag to it. Under her instructions he wrote to Mrs. Eldan, 6 Harrison Street, Liverpool on it and he secured it to the box. She appeared to be on her own at the shop and paying Mr. Westhead the sum of 1s 4d, she left with the paper-covered box.

A few minutes later, further down Friargate at the Hoop and Crown public house, Henry Hall, a labourer, of Kirkham Street, was approached by a respectably-dressed lady, who enquired if he would take a parcel for her to the railway station.

He agreed to take the trunk for a payment of threepence and she informed him that he must carry it steadily and deliver it to the parcel office.

Henry Hall carried out the errand and it was duly despatched to Liverpool on the train leaving Preston at half-past-three. By five o'clock the train was in Liverpool's Lime Street Station and the box was in due course sent out by the parcel van to be delivered to the address it bore. The porter in charge of the van could not find a Mrs. Eldan at the address shown on the label; a person named Regan was living there. He was about to take the box back to the station, when Regan informed him that he thought a Mrs. Melville, living at 6 Court, Harrison Street, would be the person for whom the box was intended. The van driver, however, would not leave the box and took it back to the railway station, saying that the woman it was directed to must apply for it there.

Mrs. Melville was told by Regan what had occurred and she remarked that she was expecting a present from some relatives in Preston. The following morning, at eleven o'clock, she went to the railway station and received the box in the name of Eldan, saying she was often called by that name in the street in which she lived.

Taking the box home with her, she called a man named Moran, who occupied a front apartment in the house and asked him to lend her a key so that she might unlock the box. He opened the box for her and when they looked inside they saw a full grown and very fine male child. Mrs. Melville thought the child was still alive and sat warming it in front of the fire, while the man informed the police.

The child was then taken to the Northern Dispensary where it was examined by the house surgeon who pronounced it dead.

The following morning two officers from Liverpool were instructed to travel to Preston and with the body of the child, its clothing and the box appeared at the police station to see Superintendant Gibbons. Once they had communicated the nature of their errand the Chief Constable of Preston at once rendered them every assistance by sending out officers in all directions. Gradually the woman's movements were pieced together and when a description of the woman was circulated, the constable from Much Hoole became suspicious that the person being sought was a woman from his village. He immediately informed his superior officer Sergeant Whiteside, who was stationed at Penwortham and after making inquiries in the vicinity of the suspect's home the sergeant was convinced they had found the woman concerned.

Without hesitating, he then went to the Much Hoole home of Jonathan Martindàle, a farm labourer, and asked to see his step-daughter Jane Parker. He told her that he was intending to apprehend her on suspicion of sending her newly-born male child in a box to Liverpool. The officer had barely finished speaking when the woman went to a cupboard in the kitchen, and taking out a small bottle attempted to drink the contents. After she had swallowed about a teaspoonful of the liquid the sergeant prevented her taking anymore and when he examined the bottle he saw a label on it marked 'laudanum'.

Jane Parker was immediately brought to Preston in a covered conveyance and taken into custody by Chief Constable Gibbons. she was told that she was charged with having murdered her child to which she made no response, appearing in fact to be particularly poorly. Obviously not fit to be questioned she was put to bed apparently suffering the effects of the laudanum she had swallowed and from a cold which she had contracted on her journey back to Much Hoole, on foot, so soon after her confinement.

The following day however Supt. Gibbons quizzed her at her bedside and she responded by saying: "I never intended to kill the child; the box has been wrongly directed and should have gone to Mrs. Parker, residing in Bute Street". She also said that she had been suffering from a bowel complaint, which had prevented her from going to see the child and that she had given it some gin to make it sleep. Adding that she had been told by a traveller that the child would live two days in a box.

When the inquest into the baby's death was held on Monday the charge from one of murder to the lesser one of manslaughter and to this indictment Jane Parker pleaded "Guilty".

In sentencing her His Lordship observed that the prisoner was a person more advanced in years than he had usually to deal with in cases of that kind. Generally speaking, they were young, unfortunate girls, who were ashamed of their acts, but she was a person who could not have that excuse. She must have been aware that to put a child in a box, as she did, and send it to Liverpool, the probabilities were that it would die. this was a very unusual thing and he could not overlook such an offence. He dared say she did not wish the child should die, probably she wished it to live; but notwithstanding that, no reasonable person could doubt that the result would be what it was.

He then announced that she must be imprisoned for a period of six months, and kept to hard labour.

'Riot Act' Read in Lune Street

SATURDAY, 13th August, 1842, is probably the date most readily recalled by those who study the history of Preston. It was on that day a disturbance took place in Lune Street that left the town in a state of anger and shock. The inhabitants of Preston witnessed a scene of slaughter not seen since the Civil Wars, when the soldiers of the Queen came into conflict with the people.

The trouble had arisen because people felt that by the introduction of machinery, which practically did away with handloom weaving, together with the repeated reductions in the wages of the factory workers throughout the country, their living would soon be gone. At that time people generally worked from six o'clock in the morning until half past seven at night and a family's wage was so small that many were living in constant fear of being turned out of their homes.

Labour was then at the mercy of capital, and working men could not endure any longer the hunger and fear of its consequences. Rioting was taking place in many Lancashire towns, and on the tragic weekend in August, 1942, Preston became the focus of attention. Many operatives came from other towns and paraded the streets in a defiant attitude. They went from mill to mill demanding the stoppage of the machinery and the setting of the workers to liberty. Regarding the machinery as a curse to humanity, the mob's purpose was to break up the power looms as they forced their way into many factories. Plugs were drawn from boilers, letting off steam and water; some of the mill gates were barricaded on the inside, and stormed from the outside; brickbats, stones and pieces of iron were thrown over the gates by the mob.

Throughout Friday, 12th August, the mill hands of Preston turned out in their thousands and that night gathered for a meeting in Chadwick's Orchard, where now the covered market stands. Various speakers from the Chartist movement addressed the gathering. The authorities, being aware of riots also taking place in Manchester, Oldham and other places, despatched a message for the military, and as a precaution decided to mount the cannon and take other means to place the House of Correction in a state of defence. Magistrates sat at the Bull Inn till a late hour, and a detachment of the 72nd Highlanders were under arms during the whole of the night.

At about six o'clock the following morning an attack was made upon a factory in North Road with the crowd calling upon the hands to turn out. Instead of complying with the order, some of the men in the factory turned the water pipes upon the mob and endeavoured to beat them back. Unfortunately they were not sufficiently strong and after some damage had been done to the outside of the mill, the hands were obliged to 'turn out'. The mob then visited a number of other mills and their ranks swelled as more operatives turned out.

Notice of these proceedings were given to the magistrates who were gathered at the Bull Inn and they determined to meet the rioters attended by the detachment of the military and the constabulary force, in the hope that they could persuade the mob to disperse.

As the time approached 8 a.m. the authorities proceeded along Fishergate and then turned down Lune Street to face the mob who lined up against them and began throwing stones. The chief constable of the county police Captain Woodford, advanced towards the crowd by himself, and strove to remonstrate with the people. While he did so a young man who appeared to be a ringleader of the rioters was waving his hand to the mob inciting them to move forward. Captain Woodford ordered him to desist and tried to capture him by seizing his collar. He missed him and within an instant had been knocked to the ground and kicked violently on the side.

The whole of the body of authority then moved down Lune Street, driving the mob before them, and chasing them through several streets, until at length both bodies came to a halt in Lune Street again. Volleys of stones were then thrown at the military and the magistrates, one part of the mob — principally women and boys — being engaged in fetching ammunition from the canal and other places where there were large piles of stones, and placing them at the feet of others.

The magistrates, the military and the constabulary were drawn-up oposite the Savings Bank, which was half way down Lune Street, and the rioters, who numbered several hundred, were below them opposite the Corn Exchange between Wharf Street and Fleet Street. The mayor, Samuel Horrocks, junior, made a strong attempt at reasoning with the parties, but with little or no effect. They were again and again told that if they did not disperse they would be fired upon.

The Mayor then read the Riot Act and as he did so a stone was thrown and knocked the document out of his hand. The riot then became more serious and alarming with no attention whatsoever being paid to the admonitions given. Then while one body of rioters followed the authorities up Lune Street, another body went up the parallel Fox Street, into Fishergate and thence to the top of Lune Street; armed with stones they then began hurling them at the authorites.

At this a sub-division of the military was ordered to face them, and they discontinued the throwing. The whole of the constabulary force, soldiers and magistrates were thus hemmed in between the two mobs. The Mayor once again attempted to reason with them, the response was the hurling of more stones and one struck the Mayor a very severe blow on the left leg.

PRESTON—ATTACK ON THE MILITARY.—

The Lune Street Riot was dramatically captured in this engraving by the Illustrated London News in 1842. Mayor Samuel Horrocks junior can be seen mounted (top left) reading the Riot Act.

At length, it was felt that not only the lives of the protective force but the safety of the town was in imminent danger and orders were given for the soldiers to fire. The mob had no idea that they would be fired upon with anything other than blank cartridges. This was an opinion shared by the spectators, including the landlord of the Corporation Arms and his family, who were watching from the windows of their public house which faced the military.

A volley was then fired above the heads of the crowd, after which John Mercer, a 27-year-old handloom weaver of Ribbleton Lane, came out from the mob and took a deliberate aim at the soldiers, but was shot in the very act and whilst his arm was uplifted. He staggered to the curb stone, fell, rolled over three times, threw out his arms and lay to all appearances dead. A volley of fire followed this traumatic moment and as a result several people engaged in the riot were wounded severely. Five of them were taken to the House of Recovery, and two to their homes. Those who were most hurt were a 19-year-old youth, George Sowerbutts, a weaver who was shot in the chest, the ball having first hit his chest before coming out of his back; Bernard MacNamera, aged 17, a stripper in a local mill, who was also shot, the ball entering the lower part of his belly making a very extensive wound. Within a couple of days, both these men, who had been returned to their homes, died. At a hastily arranged inquest, the jury returned verdicts of 'Justifiable Homicide' in both cases.

The men who had been taken to the House of Recovery were William Lancaster, aged 25, a resident of Nugent Street, who had been shot in the chest; James Robert, a 21-year-old weaver, of Savoy Street, shot in the fore-arm; Bryan Hodgson, aged 36, a shoemaker, of St. Paul's Square, wounded in the lower part of his back; John Mercer, aged 27, a handloom weaver, of Ribbleton Lane, who had been shot through the chest; Lawrence Pilling, aged 21, a weaver of Moss Rose Street, who had to have a leg amputated after a ball entered his leg below the knee, smashing the bone in a frightful manner.

The chief market day came to a complete standstill, some of the market people being afraid to stand in the market, and others, who had heard of the riot on the way to the town had halted their journey. Of those who had commodities to sell, scarcely anything was purchased. People seemed to be able to do nothing else but think and talk of what had taken place.

110

The streets gradually became quieter, and there were no further appearances of rioting, although men were grouped in Chadwicks Orchard. They seemed to have no-one to lead them, added to which further military reinforcements had arrived in town, and a great number of special constables were sworn-in. The street became liberally-placarded with notices that the Riot Act had been read, and with various proclamations and exhortations to keep the peace.

A fortnight after the riot the *Preston Chronicle* brought the town's residents up-to-date with news of the death of two more of the rioters. William Lancaster had died six days after the incident, and John Mercer, the man shot whilst in the act of hurling a stone at the military,suffered for a further four days before expiring. Inquests on both men returned verdicts similar to those given at the former inquests.

According to the newspaper, the town in the past week, had assumed, in fact, and appearance, its wonted quietness. Business was being conducted in the usual manner and little was left to tell the tale of the disturbances.

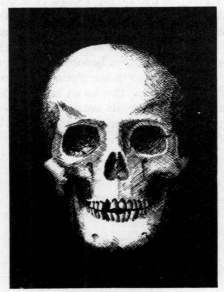

THE END